THE Gift Wrapping BOOK

THE Gift Wrapping BOOK

CAROLINE BIRKETT

David & Charles

I would like to thank the following companies for their support in the making of this book:

Paperchase at 213-215 Tottenham Court Road, London W1 9PS *for their amazing choice of art and gift wrapping papers.*
Tel: (enquiries) 020 7467 6200, (mail order) 0161 839 1500 Website: www.paperchase.co.uk

Fred Aldous *for craft papers and lots of other interesting products from paints and pens to origami paper,* all available by mail order.
Tel: 0161 236 4224 Website: www.safestreet.co.uk/fredaldous

The English Stamp Company *for stamps, paints and Mulberry paper.*
Tel: 01929 439117 Website: www.englishstamp.com

Offray *for their beautiful ribbons* which are available nationwide from needlecraft and hobby specialist shops.
Tel: 01844 258 126 or 0207 263 7311 for stockists.

Coats Crafts UK *for the edging scissors and hole cutter.*
Tel: 01325 365 857 for stockists.

A DAVID & CHARLES BOOK

First published in the UK in 2002
by David & Charles
ISBN 0 7153 1298 7 (hardback)

Distributed in North America
by F&W Publications Inc.
4700 E. Galbraith Rd.
Cincinnati, OH 45236
1-800-289-0963
ISBN 0 7153 1453 X (paperback)

EXECUTIVE COMMISSIONING EDITOR   CHERYL BROWN
EXECUTIVE ART EDITOR   ALI MYER
DESIGNER   LISA FORRESTER
DESK EDITOR   SANDRA PRUSKI
PHOTOGRAPHY   LUCY MASON

Printed in Singapore by KHL Printing Co Pte Ltd
for David & Charles
Brunel House   Newton Abbot   Devon

Contents

Introduction

The giving of gifts is at the heart of almost every type of celebration and gift wrapping has become an important part of this long established tradition. It is only since paper could be mass produced, making it an affordable, everyday material, that we have been able to indulge in this wonderfully frivolous custom. When a gift is concealed until just the right moment it creates feelings of anticipation, turning into surprise and, hopefully, delight, when the gift is finally revealed. A box with a lid is easy to open and the moment when the lid is removed to reveal the gift inside, can be quite dramatic. However, for me, nothing can beat ripping off paper and catching the first glimpse of what is enclosed. Colourful papers, ribbons and bows also create a magical atmosphere, setting the scene for a memorable day. This is particularly so at Christmas when beautifully wrapped gifts collected around the tree fill the whole room with the spirit of celebration.

In Japan it is considered discourteous to hand a person an object that is unwrapped and *Origata,* the Japanese art of gift wrapping, is governed by a complex set of rules depending on who is the recipient, the occasion, and the gift itself. Even with a more informal approach, it is still useful to think a little about the style of wrap that would be most suitable and to consider practical matters such as protecting the gift from damage.

The following pages are packed with inspirational gift wrapping ideas that are both imaginative and practical. Wrapping does not always have to be very elaborate but if it is neat and thoughtfully put together it will make a good first impression, showing the spirit in which the gift is given. A beautifully tied ribbon or hand-decorated gift box need not take long but will

always be valued by the recipient. Choose the right paper for the job from the fantastic variety that are now readily available – roughly textured or glossy, single-coloured or patterned, delicately lacy or strong and weighty. Alternatively you can make your own hand-decorated papers for unique wrapping, using one of the simple techniques shown. There are wrapping solutions for gifts that are cumbersome, along with ideas for making gift tags and tying beautiful bows.

Over 25 projects using a comprehensive collection of techniques shown with clear step-by-step photography and many more style ideas make this the only gift wrapping book you will ever need.

Natural wrapping

Concentrate on textured surfaces, using corrugated card and hand-made papers, or choose papers printed with leaf and flower motifs in shades of green. Some hand-made papers have seed-heads, leaves and flowers actually embedded in them. Brown paper can be decorated with rubbings or stamps of natural objects, or used plain with very elaborate embellishments. Crepe paper has a surface the texture of bark and is strong and flexible enough to be cut into strips and used as a tie. Raffia and hessian also make good rustic ties. Heavy, soft cotton string and thin hairy garden twine, in undyed browns as well as green, look great tied around natural papers. Use multi strands layered over another tie, or plait a number of lengths together. There are also lovely textured and linen-look ribbons or ribbons printed with leaves and other natural motifs. Decorate parcels with feathers, shells, seed-heads, leaves and sticks, which are freely available and fun to collect.

Romantic wrapping

Create some paper magic with delicate lightweight wraps and pearly finishes, or papers with hearts and flowers in the softest of colours. Tissue paper has a slight sheen and is so fine that it is almost transparent, so use a number of layers in different colours. This will create real impact when the gift is opened. Japanese lace papers are a delicate web of fibres that look beautiful layered over tissue paper of a different colour. Beautiful ribbons are essential to create a romantic mood so swathe parcels in sheer, iridescent and shot-taffeta ribbons tied in generous bows. Netting creates a cloud of colour when used as an outer wrapping or cut into strips and tied in a flamboyant bow. Shimmering crystal drops, beads and diamanté costume jewellery make precious-looking embellishments. Alternatively, a single fresh flower held in place by a simply tied ribbon is elegant and understated. A hand-made gift tag will convey your affection without the need for too many words.

Fun wrapping

A riot of colour and simple graphic prints have fabulously strong impact. Papers of all kinds in strong, solid colours can be very effective, but those with a glossy surface will enhance the intensity of saturated colour. Papers can be decorated with stickers or stamped with abstract shapes in fluorescent paints. Carry the intensity of pattern and colour through to the ribbons by using lively combinations and contrasting colours. You can buy raffia in strong, bright hues, or can even tie strips of brightly coloured fabric around the packages. Finish off with fake flowers and sweets wrapped in colourful cellophane papers – or even small toys from last year's Christmas crackers.

Hi-tech wrapping

Unusually shaped packages and papers with metallic and glossy finishes create a sleekly modern look. Hologram paper in different colours and designs are fabulous and can be tied with hologram ribbon to create a dazzling optical effect. Transparent materials like cellophane make wonderful wrap, or strips can be used to tie amazing transparent bows. Bubblewrap adds another dimension with its raised bobbly surface and it can be used in its transparent state or sprayed with metallic paint. Use it either as a wrap or to make into bags and envelopes. Metallic crepe paper also has a nicely textured surface and can be used as a wrap or a tie. Decorate hi-tech parcels with plastic mirrors, hologram stickers and structured synthetic ribbon bows.

Christmas wrapping

Create a visual feast with rich traditional colours, materials and motifs. Gold makes a good key colour as it is warm and combines well with reds, greens, blues and purples. For a really intense, reflective gold, use paper that has been hand-marbled with gold, or create your own gilded papers using gold leaf or gold pens. Printed wrapping paper featuring Christmassy images such as trees, baubles, holly and ivy inject instant Christmas cheer. For something different, conceal your gift inside a cracker, make a crepe paper Christmas stocking or stitch simple bags using sumptuous fabrics such as velvet, taffeta and lace to enclose really special gifts. Tartan ribbon is very traditional, gold ribbon is a little more glamorous, whilst tinsel, streamers and tree trim all make unusual ties. Parcels look particularly enticing when they are embellished with glittering tree ornaments, tassels, sweets and chocolate money. Alternatively, use sprigs of holly, ivy and mistletoe adorned with pine cones and berries, all materials that are traditionally used for decorating the home at Christmas time.

Perfectly Wrapped Presents

If your gift is oblong in shape, such as a book, or is in a box with squared

corners, simply wrap it in paper, as these are easy shapes to wrap neatly.

Choose a paper that is not too stiff to fold and crease. Always cut the

paper to size: excess paper can make accurate folding difficult and result

in a bulky, uneven finish. Use double-sided adhesive tape to fix it invisibly

in place. Ribbon is the final flourish so experiment with tying it around

the parcel in different ways.

• HEART-SHAPED CUT-OUTS ALLOW THE SOFTLY COLOURED TISSUE PAPER BENEATH TO SHOW THROUGH. A SHIMMERING ORGANZA RIBBON EXUDES ROMANCE

...SHLY SPOTTED PAPER IS CHEERFUL AND SUITS ANY OCCASION. CHOOSE A RIBBON TO HIGHLIGHT ONE OF THE COLOURS

• TAKE INSPIRATION FROM THE COLOURS OF A PRINTED PAPER SUCH AS THIS, AND TIE YOUR PARCEL WITH NARROW RIBBONS IN TONING SHADES

• STRONGLY CONTRASTING RIBBON TIED DIAGONALLY ACROSS THE CORNERS OF THE GIFT CREATES AN ANGULAR EFFECT THAT SUITS THE HOLOGRAPHIC PAPER

Wrapping a classic box

Straight sides and square corners make boxes simple to wrap

YOU WILL NEED:

wrapping paper

tape measure

pencil

craft knife

cutting mat

metal ruler

double-sided tape

ribbon

1 Measure the box to establish how much paper you will need. For the width of paper required, measure all round the box and add 4cm (1½in) for an overlap. For the length, measure at least two-thirds up one end, along the length and two-thirds down the other end of the box. Cut the paper to the correct size, lay it face down on a flat surface and place the box, top down, in the centre.

TIP

Ensure you have enough ribbon to go round the width and length, plus about 50cm (20in) to make a bow with nice long tails.

2 Fold under 1cm (⅜in) along the edge of the paper and apply double-sided tape along the underside. Wrap the paper around the box, ensure that it is taut, then press the tape against the face of the overlapped paper below.

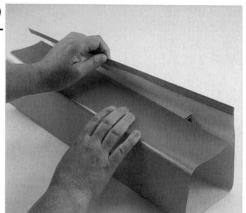

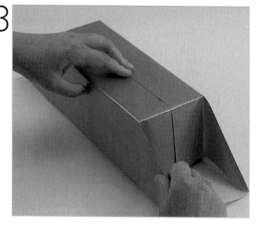

3 Centre the join on the box and centre the box inside the paper. Fold down the paper at both ends, making sure it is flat against the end of the box. Put a diagonal crease in the resulting flaps of paper at either side.

TIP

Very flat boxes are easier to wrap if the paper comes the whole way down the end of the box.

Fold in the side flaps on one end towards the
centre of the box. Crease the lower flap into
a point and put a crease along the base of the
flap so that it lays flat on the work surface.

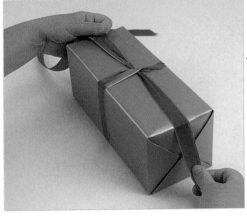

5 Apply double-sided tape near to the point of
the flap then fold it up and press it in place
against the end of the box. Repeat steps 4
and 5 for the other end of the box.

Fold the piece of ribbon in half lengthways to
find the middle and place this point centrally
on the top of the present. Take the ribbon
around either side, to meet in the centre at
the bottom.

6

7 Tie the two ends together, then take them off
at right angles and bring them back around
the other two sides to the top again.

Tie the two ends under the first band of
ribbon, and again above it, before finishing off
with a bow.

8

TIP

*Try not to rush wrapping
a present and get
everything you need to
hand before you start.
Pre-cut some pieces of
tape and keep them on
the edge of your cutting
board until they are
needed.*

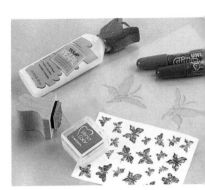

*Some decorative
techniques such as
stamping, stencilling,
relief and glitter pen, can
be applied to the paper
after it has been wrapped
around the gift. This
allows for motifs to be
spaced evenly, but be
sure to let one surface
dry before turning over
to the next.*

TIP

*Tying two knots ensures
that the bow will not be
knocked off-centre in
transit.*

Decorated and Customized Papers

Unlike permanent objects such as walls or furniture, decorated wrapping papers don't have to be perfect. A little bit of unevenness adds texture, a slightly crooked line adds character and every piece of hand decorated paper is unique. So enjoy yourself and take the opportunity to test techniques with new products such as gilding or relief paint. Use small motifs grouped closely together if the package will be a small one, a larger motif spaced openly will look better on a large present.

• SIMPLE LEAF SHAPES IN WAX RESIST ON CRUMPLED TISSUE PAPER CREATE INTRIGUING TEXTURAL EFFECTS

• DOTS OF RELIEF PAINT STAND OUT FROM THE SURFACE OF THIS PAPER LIKE TINY SHIMMERING PEARLS

• SIMPLE WHITE FLOWERS STAMPED ON SKY BLUE PAPER CREATE A FRESH AND CHARMING GIFTWRAP

• BRIGHTLY COLOURED BUTTERFLIES STENCILLED ON WHITE PAPER BRING A LIVELY, ORIENTAL INFLUENCE

Some quick and easy decorated papers

1 Wax resist

Use a candle or wax crayon to draw on white or coloured paper then paint over the top, using a darker water-based paint or ink. The wax prevents the painted colour from soaking into the paper, creating a distinctive batik effect.

2 & 8 Glitter glue and relief painting

Practice drawing your motif freehand, or cut out a simple stencil to use as a template, marking the design lightly in pencil first. Test out the product on a piece of scrap paper to stabilize the flow of the paint. Start at the top of the paper to be decorated and work towards yourself to avoid smudging. Give the product plenty of time to dry. Relief painting in a colour close to that of the paper will emphasize the texture it creates. Glitter glue will not leave a clean-edged image so to create clearly shaped motifs, mark them first with pen then roughly go over the top with the glitter.

3 Gilding

Coat the areas of paper to be gilded with a thin layer of size (a type of glue). While it is drying cut the metal leaf into squares large enough to cover your motifs. When the glue is tacky use the waxed backing paper to place the leaf on top of the glued areas, gently smoothing out any air bubbles. The leaf will adhere to the glue and remain on the paper; brush away any excess with a dry brush. Don't worry if the finish is not perfect – 'old gold' can look even more interesting.

4 Rubbings

Rubbings can be made over almost any raised surface. Look at decorative metal work, natural objects, or make your own raised patterns out of string glued to a piece of card. Choose a paper that is pliable but strong, such as sugar paper or brown parcel paper, place it over the object and rub with a wax crayon or soft pencil until an impression appears on the paper. Wax rubbings can also be used to create resist batik effects.

5 & 7 Stamping

You can use bought stamps for intricate designs or even everyday household items. (Try stamping with a cork, cut apple, bubble wrap, or corrugated card shapes to achieve some interesting effects.) Coat your chosen stamp evenly with the paint using an ink pad or special stamp paint and a roller. Press it firmly on to the paper for a few seconds. Larger stamps are generally curved and these should be rocked gently at the same time as being pressed. Keep the pressure as even as possible as you work. Re-coat the stamp before every impression.

6 Bleach painting

Paint with a mix of one part household bleach to three parts water on coloured or colour-washed paper. Within seconds the bleach will remove the colour pigments from the paper wherever it touches. Handle bleach with care, protecting your skin, clothes and work surface. Always use an acrylic paintbrush.

9 Cut and layered

Pleat up a piece of crepe paper without creasing the edges of the folds. The bigger the pleat, the more widely spaced the motifs will be. Choose a small, symmetrical design such as a diamond, heart or circle. Cut out half the design through all the layers of paper along both sides of the pleat. Open out the paper and lightly glue it over a second piece of paper in a contrasting colour.

10 Stencilling

You can buy stencils, but it is easy to make your own – see the designs on pages 106–10. Trace the design on to poster board or acetate stencil paper and with a craft knife, carefully cut out the areas where you want colour to register. Use masking tape to position the stencil on the paper and either spray or stipple paint over it with a brush lightly dipped in thick paint. Carefully remove the stencil, avoiding smudges, and reposition it for the next print.

Choosing The Right Paper

There is a stunning range of papers and cards available for gift wrapping. Don't just look at purpose-made giftwrap but consider art papers – in fact, any paper can be used if it is large and flexible enough. Paper can be reused, even if it is creased. Either iron it or crinkle it up completely and make a feature of your newly created texture. Some papers are a more suitable choice for a particular shape or size of gift than others. Choosing the right paper for the job will make wrapping much easier and more rewarding.

STICK SHEETS OF BOUGHT PAPER TOGETHER TO CREATE STRIPED PAPER BIG ENOUGH TO WRAP SOMETHING LARGE

•FOR A SOFT GIFT, FIRST WRAP WALLPAPER ROUND A SUITABLE SIZED BOOK, THEN SLIP THIS OUT AND REPLACE IT WITH YOUR GIFT BEFORE SEALING THE END

• NEWSPAPER COMES IN LARGE SHEETS SO FOR WRAPPING LARGE PRESENTS CUSTOMIZE IT WITH POTATO-STAMP DESIGNS

• CREPE PAPER IS SUITABLE FOR WRAPPING SOMETHING SOFT BECAUSE ITS PLIABILITY MAKES IT LESS LIKELY TO TEAR

Types of paper

Kraft paper (also known as parcel paper) is a strong paper with one matt and one shiny side and faint stripes running through it. Traditionally used for parcels, it is excellent for natural wrapping and can be used plain or given a decorative finish. It is inexpensive and comes in very wide sheets or rolls, making it an excellent choice for wrapping a really large present. It is most commonly brown, but is also available in different colours.

Sugar paper is a stiff coloured paper that is excellent for making bags, cones and tubes. It has quite a rough, open surface that is absorbent and takes stamps and other decorative finishes particularly well.

▶ Cardboard is stiffer than paper and although unsuitable for wrapping, is excellent for making gift boxes. There are many different weights and finishes to choose from. Alternatively, cheap cardboard can be used to back and stiffen a decorative paper for box-making.

Poster paper is an inexpensive coloured paper with a matt coloured coating on one side only. Fold it gently but precisely as the coloured surface can crack.

◀ You can buy handmade papers in different styles from around the world. They have wonderful textures with unusual effects and colours and some of the sheets can be twice the size of ordinary giftwrap. Japanese papers are soft and strong with long, visible fibres but their springiness can make them difficult to fold. Indian papers are lightweight but strong and easy to cut, though the visible flecks of plant fibre and wood can get in the way of folds.

Mulberry paper is made from the bark of the mulberry tree and has visible strands of plant fibre. It is widely available in a good range of colours and is relatively inexpensive, yet has a handmade look.

▶ Metallic paper has reflective qualities that give it a luxurious look. Crepe paper, tissue paper and brown paper are all available with a metallic finish. Foil-coated cellophane has a very glossy surface but it slips and tears easily so only use it to wrap simple shapes.

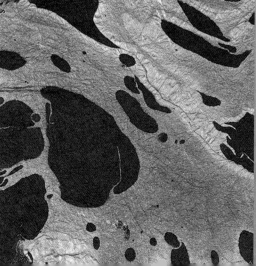

Transparent papers, such as cellophane and tracing paper can be used with an underwrapping of tissue paper to conceal the identity of the gift. Use them on hampers to protect the contents without completely concealing them.

Origami paper is made specifically for the Japanese art of paper folding. It is coated with matt colour on one side only, patterned or plain. It comes in different sizes commonly between 7.5cm (3in) and 24cm (9in) square.

▶ Crepe paper is soft and pliable with a crinkled surface. This texture makes it quite hard to fold or crease and sticky tape doesn't adhere well to it. It is excellent for wrapping circular and awkward shaped gifts as it can be shaped without tearing.

Bubble wrap is transparent plastic, layered with pockets of air trapped between. It is used as protective packing and there are a number of different bubble sizes. Greenhouse insulation looks very similar but is flat on both sides.

◀ Purchased giftwrap is available in a wide range of colours and designs and comes in sheets or rolls. The rolls generally work out less expensive and are especially useful for wrapping larger gifts.

Wallpaper can make good strong giftwrap that will protect a soft gift without tearing. It also makes great paper bags. Lining paper makes an excellent cheap base for decorative finishes.

▶ Newsprint makes an unusual giftwrap, especially foreign language newspapers with decorative script such as Chinese, Japanese or Arabic. It is a particularly good choice for wrapping a large present as it is in plentiful supply – and cheap. Newspaper can be decorated with decoupage, stamping or colour-washed with paint.

Tissue paper is lightweight but quite strong and comes in a wide range of colours including metallics. Good quality tissue paper has a sheen on its surface. It is useful under a transparent outer paper, but two or three sheets used together create a perfectly opaque wrapping on their own. It will also provide extra protection if a gift is delicate or has sharp corners.

◀ Corrugated cardboard has an undulating, ribbed surface that is both decorative and protective. It makes good cones, rolls and boxes for breakable gifts. It comes in a wide range of weights and colours.

Ribbons & Ties

Tying ribbon round a parcel may have had its origins in practicality, but today the aim is largely decorative. Nonetheless, a ribbon tied around a soft parcel will give added strength and certainly help keep its shape. Choose a ribbon that complements the colour, style, or texture of the paper – but whether your choices are understated or over the top, don't be predictable!

• HESSIAN RIBBON AND GARDEN TWINE ARE IDEAL FOR A GARDENER'S GIFT; ADD POPPY SEED HEADS FOR DECORATION

• A LAYERED BOW OF SILVER CORRUGATED CARD GIVES A NEAT, SOPHISTICATED LOOK

•TWO MULTI-LOOP BOWS BOUND TOGETHER IN A CROSS CREATE A DRAMATIC DOME-SHAPED BOW

•RIBBONS OF DIFFERENT WIDTHS AND COLOURS COMBINE FOR A GENEROUS, EXUBERANT WRAPPING

•KNOT LENGTHS OF WIRE-EDGED RIBBON TOGETHER AND CREATE A FOUNTAIN OF RIPPLING TAILS

Types of ribbon & ties

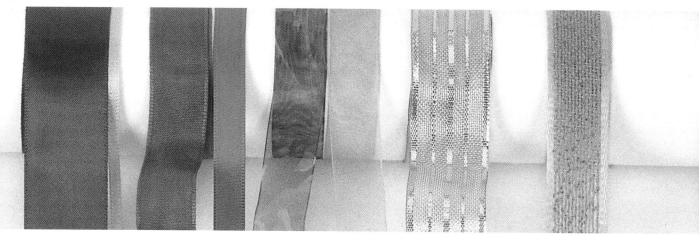

- SATIN RIBBON is woven in widths from 1.5mm (¹⁄₁₆in) to 89mm (3½in). Single-faced is shiny on one side and matt on the other; double-faced is slightly heavier and shiny on both sides. Satin ribbon is good for matching a specific shade as it comes in the widest range of colours. Shiny ribbons combine well with matt papers.

- TAFFETA RIBBON is finely woven, making it crisp to handle. It has a matt appearance on both sides and is available in plain colours, tartans and gingham check designs. The matt surface works well in neutral colours for natural wrapping. Tartans create a very traditional look for Christmas.

- SHEER RIBBON has a beautiful translucent appearance that introduces subtle colour alterations when mixed with other ribbons or laid against papers of different colours. It is very light in weight, so is easy to tie in a multi-loop bow. Use sheer ribbon on a wedding gift or a present for a new baby.

- METALLIC RIBBON has metallic yarn incorporated in its weave to achieve a whole variety of shiny, glittery or hologram-like appearances which are great for Christmas or hi-tech wrappings.

- NOVELTY RIBBONS incorporate yarns with many different characteristics to achieve a wide range of looks from natural linen to iridescent, pearlized effects.

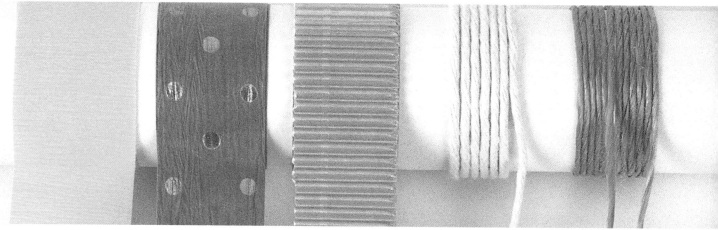

- CREPE PAPER STRIPS are strong and flexible with a textured surface. Dual colour paper ties are a different colour on each side and can be used to create interesting looped bows.

- PAPER RIBBON is available in a wide range of widths, colours and patterns. Some can be used, tightly twisted, as twine. Sometimes it can also be untwisted to create wider areas on bows.

- CORRUGATED PAPER STRIPS can be used to dress parcels and make bows. Cut the strips so that the corrugations run crosswise to give them flexibility along the length.

- COTTON STRING is soft and strong with a good creamy colour for natural wrapping. Use a single strand and a simple knot on a small present, multiple strands on larger gifts and make a pompon or multi-loop bow with it.

- NYLON STRING is available in a number of colours. It is extremely strong and has an individual texture and appearance that is particularly suitable for hi-tech wrapping.

- PRINTED RIBBON has a design printed on one side and sometimes on both. Avoid tying bows with ribbon that is printed on one side only because when it is twisted the design can't be seen. Printed designs can make wrapping more fun by introducing flashes of a bright colour or motifs.

- WIRE-EDGED RIBBON has a fine, flexible wire incorporated in its edges which retains its shape. It is perfect for making lavish bows with long undulating tails. Satin, taffeta, sheer and many other ribbons are available with a wired edge.

- CRAFT RIBBON is created by cutting a larger piece of fabric into strips. To prevent the edges fraying it is treated with a finish that makes it quite stiff. There are metallic, printed, checked and textured ribbons, available in some very wide widths. They can also have wired edges.

- SYNTHETIC RIBBON is cheap and cheerful. It is mainly used to make wonderful curled bow tails and embellishments created by running it over the blade of a pair of scissors. It is usually 0.5cm (3/16in) wide and there are some attractive iridescent effects available.

- CORDS are made in a variety of ways including knitting, plaiting and twisting. They tend to be narrow and rounded rather than flat. Metallic cord is very effective as the light catches the rounded surface.

- GARDEN TWINE is a rough tie made from jute. In both green and natural colours, it gives a rustic theme to your wrapping. Plait three strands together to make a heavier tie.

- RAFFIA is a natural material from palm tree leaves which looks like dried grass when cut into strips. It is available in its natural colour as well as in some fun colours. The length of the strips is limited to about 80cm (31in), so knot lengths together or use it on smaller presents.

- KNITTING YARN and embroidery threads are very narrow so use them to tie round smaller gifts and to attach gift tags. The types and colours are endless, so experiment with space-dyed or metallic threads and textured bouclé yarns.

- LACE can be expensive but narrow strips are affordable and make quaint, old fashioned-looking ties.
- BRAID, particularly ric-rac braid, makes a fun tie because of its unusual wavy shape.

- NETTING can be bought in strips or can easily be cut from a bigger piece as it does not fray. Be generous with the width as it is most effective when it is lightly gathered. Other types of fabric can also be used but cut them on the bias to prevent them fraying.

A classic hand-tied bow

A simple bow tied from one length of ribbon

YOU WILL NEED

80cm (31½in) of
39mm (1½in) wide
satin ribbon

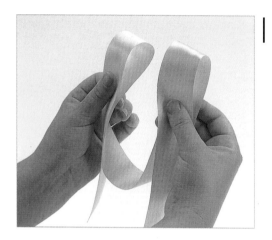

Fold the ribbon in half lengthways, then in half again, to make two evenly spaced loops. Hold one in each hand.

TIP

Save and reuse
expensive ribbon –
ironed flat, it will look
as good as new.

Fold the left loop over the right.

TIP

Cut ends of ribbon
diagonally or in a 'V'
shape to prevent
fraying.

Take the left loop round to the back of the right, then forward through the hole created in the centre. Pull the loops away from each other to tighten the centre. You may need to adjust the loops and tails to make the bow even before finally tightening.

A layered bow
This bow is constructed with a number of ribbon loops

Cut three lengths of ribbon: the first, twice the finished width of the bow plus 2cm (⅞in) overlap; the second shorter; and the third shorter again.

For this bow the lengths measured 30cm (12in), 22cm (8½in), and 10cm (4in).

YOU WILL NEED

62cm (24½in) of 39mm (1½in) wide wired ribbon

scissors

double-sided adhesive tape

ruler

Create three loops by joining the ends of each strip with double-sided tape, overlapping them by 1cm (⅜in) and making sure the join is central. On the two larger loops attach a piece of double-sided tape to the inside of the join, then flatten each loop so the top layer sticks to the tape on the lower layer.

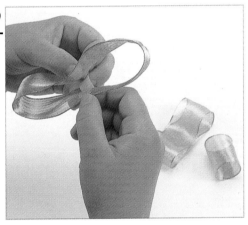

TIP

If you want to show off a very special ribbon, choose an understated paper as a background. On the other hand, if you've spent time on hand-decorating an individual paper, then a simple tie would be best.

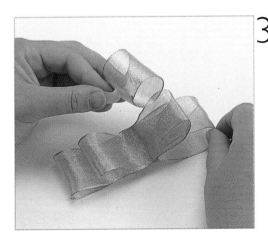

Put another piece of double-sided tape on the outside of each loop, again over the join. Stick the second loop to the centre of the first and the third to the centre of the second. Leave the cover paper on the tape on the very bottom of the bow until you want to attach it to the present.

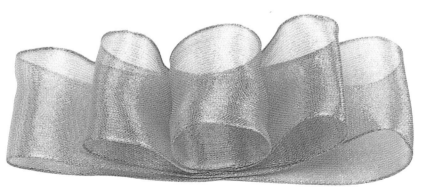

A multi-loop bow

This bow has more than two loops and is bound in the middle with wire

YOU WILL NEED

80cm (31½in) of
  39mm (1½in) wide
  wired ribbon

scissors

florist's wire

double-sided adhesive
  tape

ruler

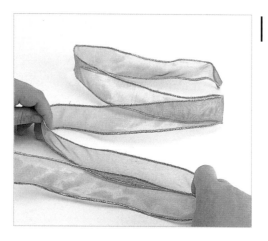

1 Set aside a 5cm (2in) length of ribbon for
finishing. Fold the rest in a continuous length
to form the required number of loops.
Illustrated is a double-loop bow.

Bind wire round the centre of the bow
to draw it in (alternatively, use some
strong thread).

2

3 Cover the wiring at the centre with the small
length of set-aside ribbon, securing it in place
on the back with double-sided tape. Open
out the loops and arrange the bow into
shape.

A ribbon rose-embellished bow

This is a multi-loop bow decorated at the centre with ribbon roses

With the narrow ribbon make a multi-loop bow about 14cm (5½in) wide (see opposite). Bind the centre with thread and leave it uncovered. To make three ribbon roses, begin by cutting the sheer ribbon into three pieces, each 40cm (16in) long. Take one piece and fold the end down diagonally.

2 Roll the first few centimetres of ribbon to make the centre of the rose, then secure it at the base with a couple of stitches.

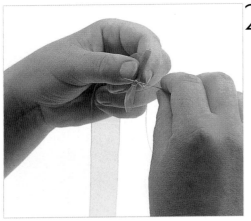

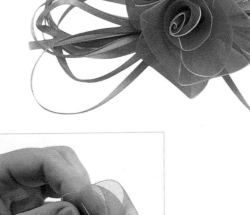

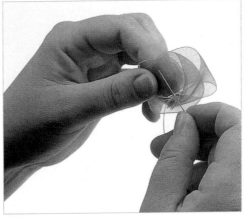

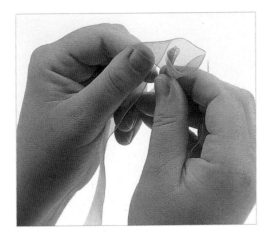

3 Start folding the ribbon outwards from the centre and diagonally forwards every few centimetres while wrapping it round the central roll. Secure it at the base with a stitch after each fold.

4 Continue folding and stitching until you reach the end of the ribbon, then fold the end diagonally down to the base and secure it with a stitch. Make two more roses and sew them to the centre of the bow.

> ## TIP
> *Ready-made roses can be bought from most haberdashery shops. As an alternative, make pompons or tassels.*

Covered Recycled Boxes

All sorts of products are bought or delivered in well-constructed, sturdy cardboard boxes and it is a shame to throw them away. Some can be dismantled and stored flat until you need them. Cover them with giftwrap or art paper, or hand decorate them. A decorative and useful box is more than just the wrapping, it becomes part of the present.

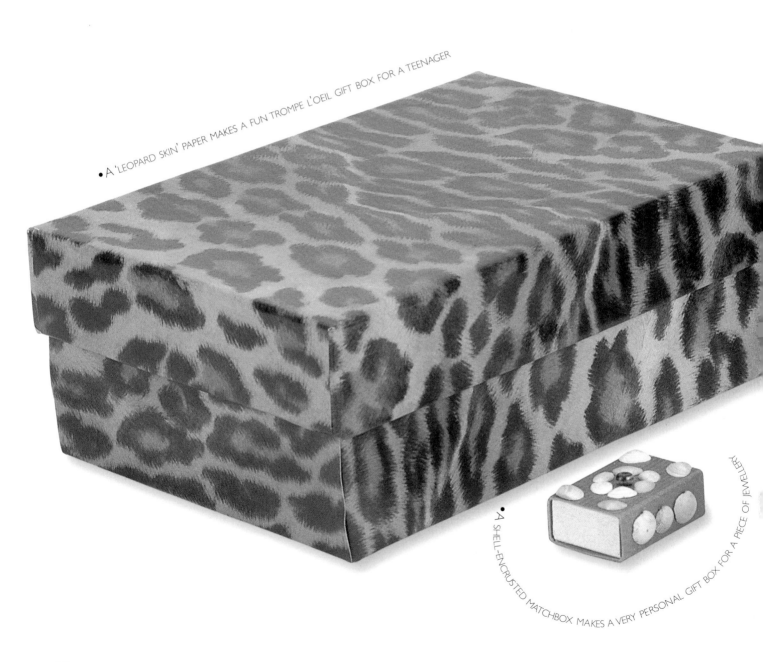

• A 'LEOPARD SKIN' PAPER MAKES A FUN TROMPE L'OEIL GIFT BOX FOR A TEENAGER

• A SHELL-ENCRUSTED MATCHBOX MAKES A VERY PERSONAL GIFT BOX FOR A PIECE OF JEWELLERY

• THIS UNUSUAL TUBULAR CONTAINER WILL KEEP ITS CONTENTS SECRET UNTIL CHRISTMAS DAY

• A SUMPTUOUS BOX WITH AN EMBOSSED LID AND TIED WITH SHOT TAFFETA RIBBON MIGHT CONTAIN THE MOST LUXURIOUS OF GIFTS

• HANDMADE PAPER INCORPORATING PRESSED LEAVES TRANSFORMS A ROUND BOX INTO A DELICATE, UNDERSTATED PACKAGE

Covering a square or oblong box

Try to match the wrapping to the contents of the box

YOU WILL NEED:

lidded box such as a
  shoe box

paper

tape measure

pencil and clear ruler

craft knife

cutting mat

metal ruler

spray adhesive

A square of textured wallpaper creates an embossed effect then enamel spray paint gives a dense, even coating of colour if applied in a succession of light coats.

1 Measure the box base and lid separately. The length of paper required for the base is twice the height plus the length of the box, plus about 2cm (¾in) to turn in for a neat edge. The width is twice the height plus the width of the box, again plus at least 2cm (¾in). Calculate the size of paper required for the lid in the same way. Cut the two pieces of paper to the correct sizes.

With the smaller piece face down, centre the box lid. Lightly draw two lines at right angles to each other from each box corner to the edge of the paper. On the front and back add 1cm (⅜in) to make neat corners. Trim away excess paper then cut slits from the edge down to each corner of the box, so that the 1cm (⅜in) allowances create small flaps. 2

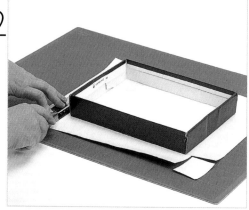

3 Spray adhesive on the reverse of the paper and replace box in the centre. At the front and back, fold the paper and press it in place up the sides and down inside the lid. Fold the corner flaps round onto the ends.

4 Fold up and press the paper in place on the ends and inside the lid, covering the flaps from the front and back. Repeat the whole process for the base.

Covering a round box

Achieving a smooth finish is simplicity itself

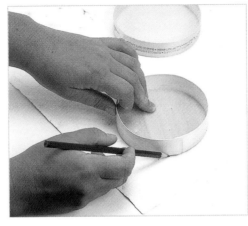

YOU WILL NEED:

an old box such as a
   camembert or truffle
   box

paper

tape measure

pencil and clear ruler

craft knife

cutting mat

metal ruler

scissors

spray adhesive

1 Measure for the strip of paper to wrap round the box base. Its width will be the depth of the box and its length the circumference plus 1cm (⅜in) for an overlap. Draw it on the reverse of the paper and cut it out. Lay the paper face down and place the box base on top. Draw lightly around the base then draw a second line by eye, 1cm (⅜in) outside the first. Cut out a circle following this outer line.

2 Make cuts into the outer edge of the circle as far as the inner circle, as if creating a fringe. Spray the reverse of both pieces of paper with adhesive.

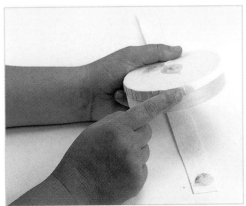

3 Stick the circular piece centrally to the box base, then smooth the fringed edges around onto the side.

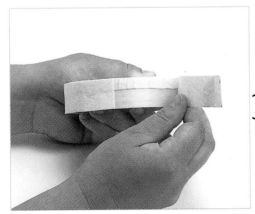

4 Stick the strip of paper around the box side, so that the edges are aligned and the 'fringe' covered. Repeat the process for the lid. Your circular covered box is now ready to be filled.

TIP

You can use the same technique in heavier card to make a circular box from scratch.

Use pictures from Christmas magazines and catalogues to cover Christmas gift boxes. Simply cut a strip to go round the tube and a disc to fit into the lid.

Hinged and Lidded Boxes

Hinged boxes are very quick and easy to make as they are constructed from a single piece of card. They are so easy to assemble, you can prepare a number of boxes in different styles and sizes and store them flat, then quickly assemble them when you need one. Lidded boxes are more complex, so take a little longer to make, but they are also more durable and look more luxurious. It is worth spending time on making boxes as they can be used afterwards for storage and display or even used again for gift giving.

ADD SPARKLE TO YOUR GIFT BOX WITH A STAR-SHAPED LID IN RADIANT HOLOGRAM PAPER

CREATES A BOX THAT COMBINES DELICACY AND STRENGTH

JAPANESE LACE PAPER LAYERED OVER COLOURED CARD

CREATE AN AIR OF MYSTERY WITH A RICHLY ORNAMENTAL BOX DECORATED WITH AN INTRICATE LACE PATTERN

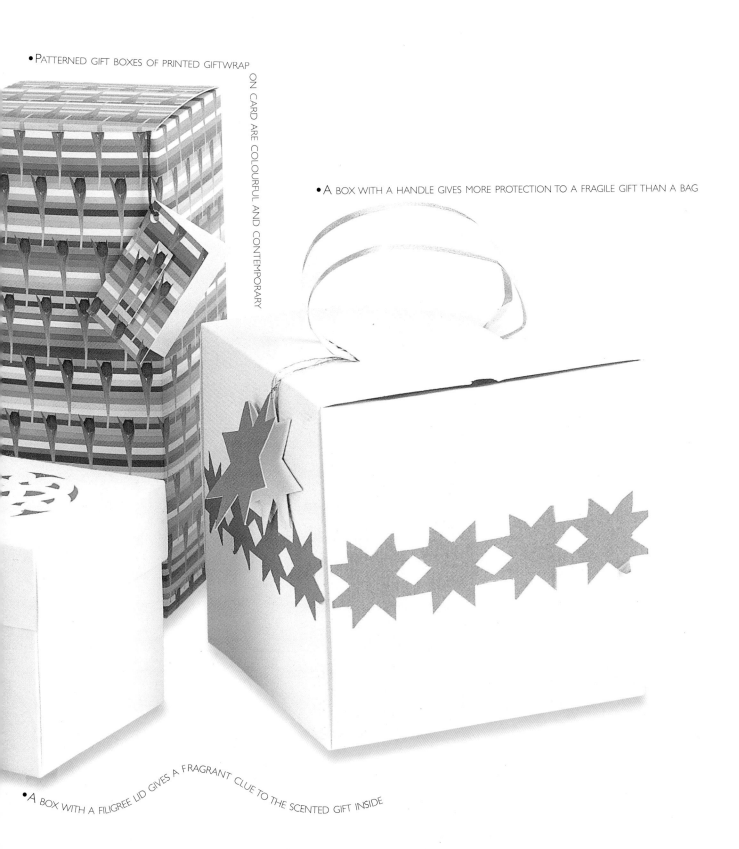

• Patterned gift boxes of printed giftwrap

on card are colourful and contemporary

• A box with a handle gives more protection to a fragile gift than a bag

• A box with a filigree lid gives a fragrant clue to the scented gift inside

Making a box with a lid
Start with the simplest style of box

YOU WILL NEED:

medium weight
  cardboard

glue

craft knife

metal ruler

cutting mat

scoring tool

pencil

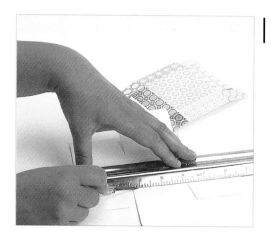

1 Copy the templates on page 100, scaling them up as necessary. Transfer the templates to the reverse of your chosen card and cut out, using a craft knife and metal ruler. Working on the reverse, lightly score all the fold lines shown on the template and create a valley fold where there is a dashed line (see page 99).

Fold up sides 1 and 2 with flaps and then fold the flaps in at right angles to form a square. 2

TIP

Experiment with making lids and bases in contrasting colours or patterned and plain card.

3 Apply glue all over the reverse of sides 3 and 4 and fold them upwards, pressing them into position over the first two flaps.

Tuck the tabs at the top 4 over the edge, pressing them firmly into place on the inside of the box. Repeat the whole process to make the lid. Your lidded box is now ready to be filled.

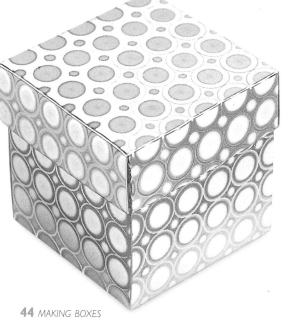

Adding a filigree design
This makes the perfect addition for a scented gift

Make a copy of the design on page 108 scaling it up as necessary. If you are tracing the design, it is only necessary to draw the design on one side of the tracing paper.

YOU WILL NEED:

scalpel knife

tracing paper

pencil

masking tape

cutting mat

2 After the box shape is cut out but still flat, position the design with masking tape on the face of the card, centred on the lid top. Cut through both the copy of the design and the card, following the lines accurately. Lift away the template and carefully remove all the unwanted areas of card. Continue making up as described on page 44.

TIP

It is particularly important that the blade of your knife is sharp for intricate cutting such as this.

To turn a square box into a star box, cut an extra piece of card in the shape of a star and glue it to the lid. Form a star template by cutting two squares the same size as the lid and gluing one on top of the other at 45º.

Making a self-hinged box
The quickest, simplest box you can make

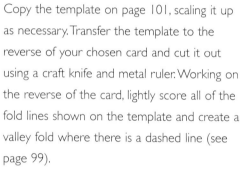

YOU WILL NEED:

medium weight cardboard

glue

craft knife

metal ruler

cutting mat

scoring tool

pencil

TIP

These boxes are so easy to assemble, you can prepare several in different styles and sizes and store them flat but ready scored. When needed, you can quickly assemble one.

Gummed shapes are a simple way to add bold pattern and colour to a plain box.

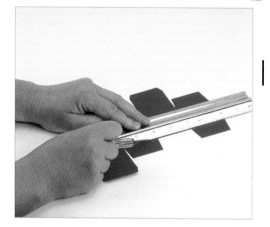

1 Copy the template on page 101, scaling it up as necessary. Transfer the template to the reverse of your chosen card and cut it out using a craft knife and metal ruler. Working on the reverse of the card, lightly score all of the fold lines shown on the template and create a valley fold where there is a dashed line (see page 99).

2 Form the box shape. Cover the face of the side join flap with glue and press it under the edge of the side panel at the other end, whilst aligning the top edges, sides and base fold lines.

3 Construct the base of the box. First fold in the two side flaps followed by the base flap, tucking up the end tab into the slit created at the back. You can apply glue all over the face of the side flaps to make the box more permanent but you will then be unable to disassemble it and store it flat.

Adding a handle

When adding a handle, turn the box on its side so that the top and base flaps form two of the vertical sides

1 Cut out the box shape as described opposite. Whilst it is still flat, reinforce the area where the handle will be attached by gluing a piece of card to the reverse of what will be the top of the box.

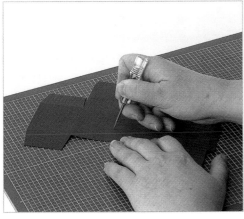

2 Pierce two holes with a bradawl, from the face to the reverse for a cord handle, or cut two slits for a ribbon handle. They should be centralized within the box top and about 8cm (3⅛in) apart for a box carried with the whole hand, closer together for a tiny box carried with a couple of fingers.

Thread the ribbon or cord up through one slit or hole and back down through the other. Tie the two ends of the ribbon together, or knot the ends of heavy cord individually.

To create a 'star chain' begin by cutting a piece of paper to the same depth as your design (see page 106 for the star template), and to whatever length you require. Fold the paper concertina-style in the same way as in 'Making a paper fan bow' (see page 90) with pleats the same width as the width of the design. Cut out the design through all the layers of paper, taking care to leave areas intact along the folds. Unfold to reveal a continuous strip of shapes.

To add the metallic stencil design to your box you will need spray paint and a paper doily. After the box shape has been cut out but is still flat, position the doily on each side of the box in turn, protecting the rest of the box with newspaper. Spray with metallic paint, allowing the paint to dry completely on each section before moving on to the next. Continue making up the box as usual.

TIP

The larger the box you wish to make, the heavier the card you should use.

Shaped Boxes

Even if the gift inside is a little 'everyday', the box doesn't have to be! These pyramid and hexagonal boxes are instantly eye-catching and will conceal the shape of the gift inside. The hexagonal box is perfect for circular gifts and the pyramid box could be filled with stones and used as a paperweight afterwards. Self-closing boxes look complicated but are in fact quite easy to make. The closing mechanism is simple but neat, and the interlocked tabs on the top have a decorative rosette-like appearance.

• RICHLY PATTERNED PAPER FOLDS INTO A VERY DRAMATIC ROSETTE WHEN CLOSED

• GRAPHITE CARD EMBELLISHED WITH GLINTING GOLD SQUARES MAKES THIS HEXAGONAL BOX SERIOUSLY GLAMOROUS

AN ANGULAR SHAPE AND DARKER COLOURS MAKE THIS LARGE PYRAMID A VERY MASCULINE GIFT BOX

A BIG, SHOWY BOW ADDS A TOUCH OF FRIVOLITY TO A SIMPLE OCTAGONAL BOX

•HEAVY HANDMADE PAPER INCORPORATING FLOWER PETALS CREATES A SIMPLE, DELICATE BOX TO HOUSE A FRAGILE GIFT

Making a pyramid box

This intriguing shape will always invite attention

YOU WILL NEED:

heavy tracing paper

glue

craft knife

metal ruler

cutting mat

scoring tool

pencil

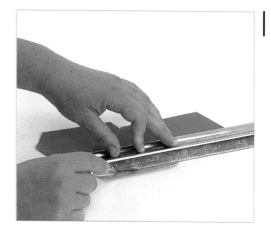

1 Copy the template on page 103, scaling it up to the required size. Transfer it to the reverse of your chosen card and cut out using a craft knife and metal ruler. Working on the reverse, lightly score all of the fold lines shown on the template and create a valley fold where there is a dashed line *(see page 99)*.

The same template enlarged to different sizes will make boxes to take gifts both large and small.

Form the box shape. Cover the face of the side join flap with glue and press it in place under the adjacent edge which has no flap, aligning the fold with the edge. Your pyramid box is now ready to be filled. 2

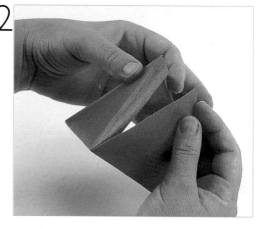

3 When closing your box, fold down the remaining flap, tuck the two tabs inside the box and lock it in place by slipping the protruding strip of paper into the slit opposite.

Making a hexagonal box
Unusual-shaped boxes are easier to make than it seems

Copy the template on page 105, scaling it up to the required size. Transfer it to the reverse of your chosen card and cut out using a craft knife and metal ruler. Working on the reverse, lightly score all the fold lines shown on the template and create a valley fold where there is a dashed line *(see page 99)*.

YOU WILL NEED:

medium weight card

glue

craft knife

metal ruler

cutting mat

scoring tool

pencil

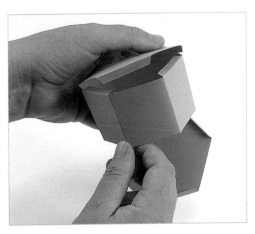

2 Form the box shape. Cover the face of the side join flap with glue and press it in place under the edge at the opposite end. Carefully align the top edges, sides and base fold lines.

3 Form the box base. Apply glue to the face of all the tabs on the base, then fold in the side tabs followed by the hexagonal flap, tucking its tabs inside the box. Press all the tabs firmly into place. Your hexagonal box is now ready to be filled. To close the lid, repeat this step, but without the glue.

Add this gilded detail to the box after it has been cut out and scored, but whilst it is still flat. Apply squares of gold leaf to each side of the box in the usual way (see page 24), then stick a smaller square of card in the centre of each gilded square.

Making a self-closing box
This makes a surprisingly secure package

YOU WILL NEED:

medium weight card

tissue paper

glue

spray adhesive

craft knife

scissors

metal ruler

cutting mat

scoring tool

pencil

1 Crumple up a piece of tissue paper slightly larger than the card you wish to cover, then lightly coat one side of the cardboard with spray adhesive, following the manufacturer's instructions.

With the tacky side of the cardboard facing up, smooth the tissue paper on to the card, allowing some wrinkles to form. The amount and size of the wrinkles can be controlled by pulling the tissue paper more or less taut.

3 Copy the template on page 102, scaling it up as necessary. Transfer the template to the reverse of your chosen card and cut it out using a craft knife and metal ruler for the straight edges and scissors for the curves. Working on the reverse of the card, lightly score all of the fold lines shown on the template and create a mountain fold where there is a dotted line and a valley fold where there is a dashed line (see page 99).

4 Next, form the box shape. Cover the face of the side join flaps with glue and press them under the side edge of the back panel, at the same time aligning the top edges, sides and base fold lines.

5 Now construct the base of the box. This does not require glue. Fold in the flap with the cut out oblong shape first, then the two diagonally cut flaps. The triangular shape on the final flap locks securely into the hole created by the first three flaps. Your self-closing box is now ready to be filled.

TIP

To attach a gift tag, anchor the thread inside the box and allow the tag to come up through the hole in the centre.

To close this box just interlock the top by squeezing the pieces together whilst twisting slightly. 6

Making an origami box

Use this ancient art to make striking modern boxes that are perfect for small gifts such as jewellery

YOU WILL NEED:

piece of 23cm (9in) origami paper to make a box with a base of 8.5cm(3⅜in) square, or

piece of 12.5cm (5in) origami paper to make a box with a base of 4.5cm(1¾in) square

1 Working on the reverse of the paper, create a mountain fold (see page 99) horizontally and vertically across the centre, unfolding each time before making the next crease. Then fold each corner to the centre.

Keeping the corners folded in, fold each edge to the centre point, unfolding each time before making the next crease. 2

3 Open out two opposite corners and re-crease the valley folds running parallel to the sides.

TIP

You could use good quality wrapping paper to make origami boxes. To make a perfect square, take one of the corners of one of the short edges and fold it diagonally across to the long edge. Cut across the paper along the edge of the triangle this creates.

4 Make the paper stand up by bringing the points diagonally either side of the corner to meet in the centre of the fold running between them.

TIP

Accurate folding is particularly important, especially the early folds. So always fold on a hard surface and take care that the paper is properly aligned.

5 Lock the end of the box by folding the corner over the top and into the centre. Repeat steps 4 and 5 to create the other end of the box. Your origami box is now ready to be filled.

When using a single box, cover the gift with tissue paper or cellophane and tie it in with ribbon. For a box with a lid, make two, with one box slightly smaller than the other.

Paper Gift Bags

A gift bag is an elegant and practical wrapping when delivering a present by hand. Paper for making bags must be fairly robust, so in addition to the usual giftwraps why not consider using a colourful wallpaper, traditional brown parcel or sugar paper? A lining paper in a contrasting colour will bring added surprise while your choice of ribbons and threads for the ties will give the finishing touch.

A PIERCED PAISLEY DESIGN ON THIS SUGAR PAPER BAG ADDS A FEMININE TOUCH

HOLOGRAM PAPER IS MODERN, EYE-CATCHING AND MAKES STRONG, DURABLE GIFT BAGS

• A TRANSLUCENT BAG OF COLOURED TRACING PAPER ENTICES YOU TO UNTIE THE RIBBON AND DISCOVER WHAT'S INSIDE

• A PARCEL PAPER GIFT BAG SUITS RUSTIC HANDLES OF PLAITED STRING. THE BUNDLE OF FRESH HERBS IS A CLUE TO THE GIFT INSIDE — INFUSED OILS

• A MINI BAG WITH RIBBON HANDLES IS THE PERFECT PRESENTATION FOR A SMALL GIFT

Making a bag

You can make the handle from cord, ribbon or twine

YOU WILL NEED

medium weight
  decorative paper

2 small pieces of
  lightweight card

cord or ribbon

glue

craft knife

cutting mat

metal ruler

hole punch

scoring tool

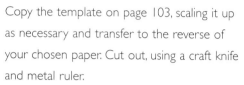

1 Copy the template on page 103, scaling it up as necessary and transfer to the reverse of your chosen paper. Cut out, using a craft knife and metal ruler.

    Working on the reverse side, lightly score all fold lines shown on the template creating a mountain fold where there is a dotted line and a valley fold where there are dashed lines (see *Basic Techniques*, page 99).

Glue strips of lightweight card to the reverse of the facing as shown, to reinforce the areas where the handles will go. Fold down the facing along the top edge of the bag and glue it in position. 2

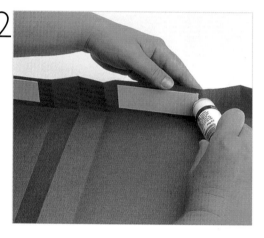

3 Form the bag shape. Cover the face of the side join flap with glue and press it under the side edge of the back panel. Make sure to align the top edges, sides and base fold lines.

To make a cut handle, increase the depth of the facing by 50 per cent. Use the template on page 111 and mark the handle shape in the same position on both the front and back of the bag. Cut away the unwanted paper with a craft knife.

TIP

If your chosen paper is too lightweight, line it with another paper while still flat, using spray adhesive. Allow it to dry thoroughly. Even a delicate tissue paper can be extremely strong if used together with wall lining paper.

4 Construct the base. Apply glue to the face of the side flaps along the bottom edge and all over the reverse of the front and back flaps. First fold in the side tabs, then the front and back flaps, and press in place.

If necessary, reinforce the base by cutting a piece of card to the same dimensions and gluing it firmly inside.

Form the side pleats. Press the front and back of the bag together so that the paper folds inwards along the pre-scored lines.

5

TIP

Shredded coloured tissue paper, cellophane or bubble wrap can be fun as well as protecting delicate items.

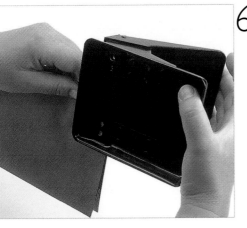

6 With a hole punch make two holes on both the front and back of the bag at least 1cm (⅜in) down from the upper edge and between a quarter and a third of the width in from each side.

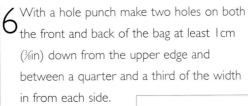

TIP

When deciding on the size of your bag, allow a little space for protective packaging.

Cut two pieces of cord or ribbon long enough for the handles plus attachment. To thread the cord, start from inside the bag, bring it up through one hole and back down through the other hole on the same side. For heavy cord, knot the ends individually; with ribbon, tie the ends together to create a continuous loop.

7

For a bag that ties closed, thread the ribbon straight through from front to back, then via the other holes through from back to front. Tie the two ends together at the front to make a pretty bow.

To add the pierced paisley design to a bag, make a copy of the design on page 108. After the bag has been cut out but is still flat, use masking tape to place the design centrally on the reverse of the front panel. Lay over a piece of soft wood and pierce through both layers with a bradawl, following the lines of the design.

Fabric Bags

You don't need to be an experienced stitcher to make a gift bag from almost any fabric as only a few straight lines of stitching are needed. Use all sorts of different leftover fabrics to create bags with very different looks. If you don't have a sewing machine, simply sew the seams by hand.

• GINGHAM CHECKS WITH FABRIC PEN 'CROSS STITCH' DECORATION CREATE A STRONG COUNTRY STYLE

• A CHAMBRAY BAG, TIED WITH RAFFIA AND DECORATED WITH A FRAYED FLOWER PATCH HAS A CHEERFUL AIR

A PLUSH VELVET BAG TRIMMED WITH GOLD TASSELS AND EMBELLISHMENTS WOULD LOOK FABULOUS UNDER ANY CHRISTMAS TREE

A TRANSLUCENT ORGANZA BAG GIVES JUST AN ENTICING GLIMPSE OF THE CHOCOLATES INSIDE

Making a fabric bag

Choose a fabric that will keep to the theme of your gift

YOU WILL NEED

fabric

sewing thread

a needle or sewing machine

ribbon

iron

scissors

tape measure

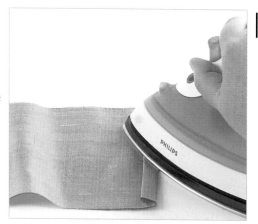

Cut a piece of fabric 3cm (1¼in) wider than the finished dimensions and twice the length plus 6cm (2⅜in). Fold the fabric in half lengthways with wrong sides together and iron in a crease. Fold in 1.5cm (⅝in) then 1.5cm (⅝in) again along both of the ends and iron in the creases.

Make your own decorative patch. Cut out a square of calico and fray around the edges. Using a fabric pen, draw the flower design shown on page 109. Iron it to fix the design, then attach it to the bag with iron-on adhesive webbing.

Fold the fabric in half with right sides together and stitch up the sides, 1.5cm (⅝in) in from the edge.

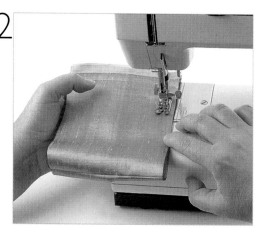

Turn the bag right side out, then fold the fabric under along the pre-ironed lines and stitch around the opening to create a double hem. Your fabric bag is now ready to be filled. Tie a length of ribbon around its neck to secure the gift inside.

Attach a shop-bought sequin motif with iron-on adhesive webbing. Turn the bag inside out and iron from the reverse of the fabric.

TIP

These pretty bags can be used afterwards to hold sweet-smelling lavender.

Circular fabric sachet

This type of sachet is often used to enclose wedding favours

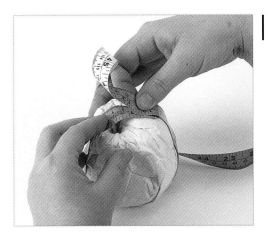

1 To establish the size of the fabric you will need, measure round the gift at its widest point (twice the height plus twice the width) and add 20cm (8in) to the measurement. This is the length and width of the fabric

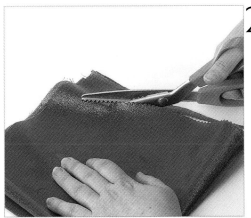

2 Cut it out and fold it in half, then in half again. Trim the unfolded edges into an arc with pinking shears so that when the fabric is unfolded it is roughly circular

Sew a line of running stitch around the circle, 10cm (4in) in from the edge. Start and finish on the right side of the fabric, leaving just a small length of thread at each end.

3

4 With the fabric right side down, place the gift in the centre of the circle and then tie the ends of the embroidery thread and tighten them to gather the fabric up around the gift. Finish with a bow.

Making a heart-shaped sachet

Soft, pliable papers can be treated almost in the same way as woven fabrics and made up as ornamental sachets with the stitching replaced by staples

YOU WILL NEED

crepe paper

lace paper

stapler

scissors

ribbon

pencil

1 Copy the template on page 108 scaling it up to the required size. Transfer the template to the reverse of the papers and with the scissors, cut out three hearts from the crepe paper and one from the lace paper.

2 Layer the four pieces with the lace paper on top, lining up the edges. Staple them together 1cm (⅜in) in from the edge, spacing the staples as evenly as possible. Leave a gap big enough to put your gift inside.

3 Place the gift inside with two layers of paper on either side. Ensuring that the gift is clear of the edge, carefully staple the sachet closed. Finish with a bow and tag.

The mini stockings are made in the same way but with the template reduced instead of enlarged. Fill them with mini goodies such as bath pearls, cufflinks or earrings, or hang them on the tree filled with candy.

TIP

Cut a stencil and spray the recipient's name across the cuff of their stocking

Create some instant Christmas magic with this crepe paper stocking decorated with stencilled gold stars. It is made in the same way as the heart sachet but along the top edge the two front and two back layers are stapled together separately to create an opening. Now it just needs filling with presents. The templates for the stocking and the star stencil can be found on page 106.

TIP

Parcel paper or wallpaper would also be strong enough to make small stockings

Making an envelope

Vouchers and money are very welcome gifts, but they can sometimes seem a little unexciting on the day. A decorative envelope will help to make the gift more special

YOU WILL NEED

paper

glue

craft knife

cutting mat

metal ruler

scissors

scoring tool

decorative materials

pencil

1 Copy the template on page 107 scaling it up as necessary. Transfer the template to the reverse of the paper and cut it out using a craft knife and metal ruler for the straight lines and scissors for the curves. On the reverse, lightly score all of the fold lines shown on the template and create a valley fold where there is a dashed line *(see page 99)*.

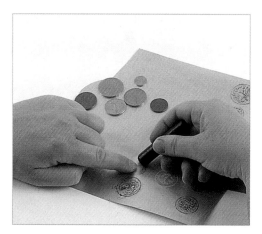

2 Now apply the decorative effect you want, such as rubbings or decoupage.

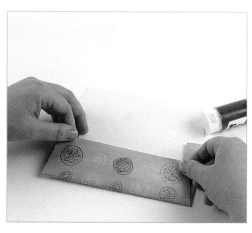

3 Form the envelope shape. Apply glue along the reverse of the side edges on the bottom flap. Fold in the side flaps first, followed by the bottom flap, pressing it into position on top. Your envelope is now ready to be filled. To seal it closed, fold down the top flap and use a decorative sticker or a dab of glue to hold it in place.

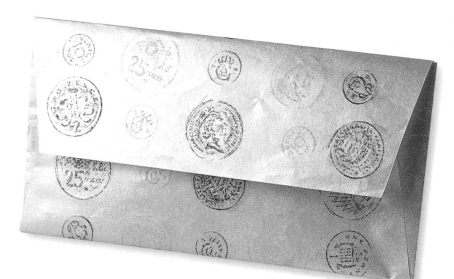

An unwanted manuscript, or a photocopy of a piece of music, makes the perfect envelope for a music voucher. Paint it with a wash of tea to give it a more intriguing aged look.

An envelope covered with a patchwork of pictures from an old seed catalogue attractively conceals garden vouchers. Why not include an inexpensive packet of seeds too, for some instant interest?

You can make mini envelopes in exactly the same way to use as tags – slip a card with a private message inside

Bubble Wrap

You've probably used bubble wrap for protection when wrapping something fragile but have you ever considered its decorative qualities? The series of ordered circles or bubbles create a wonderfully textured surface with a hi-tech look. Next time, instead of using it on the inside, why not put it on the outside of your parcel? It will also serve as a visual reminder to handle the parcel with care.

• PRINTING WITH BUBBLE WRAP CREATES AN INTERESTING HONEYCOMB PATTERN

• CLEAR CELLOPHANE TIES MAKE A SUITABLY SLEEK ADDITION TO THE BUBBLE WRAP THEME

• A SILVER BUBBLE WRAP ENVELOPE WITH HOLOGRAPH EDGING MAKES A PRACTICAL AND STYLISH WRAP FOR A CD

• A TACTILE BUBBLE WRAP BAG WILL CUSHION AND CONTAIN A SINGLE ITEM OR A COLLECTION OF SMALLER GIFTS

• AN UNUSUAL BUBBLE WRAP BOW ADDS DRAMATIC IMPACT TO BUBBLE WRAPPING

Making a bubble wrap envelope
Using holographic adhesive tape maintains the space-age look

YOU WILL NEED

bubble wrap

metallic spray paint

craft knife

cutting board

metal ruler

holographic adhesive
tape

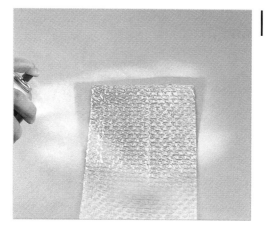

1 Cut a piece of bubble wrap twice the length of the gift plus 6cm (2⅜in) and to the width of the gift plus 2cm (¾in). Spray the right side silver with metallic paint and leave it to dry.

With the silver side down, measure 4cm (1⅝in) from the top edge and fold the other end over and up to this point. The 4cm (1⅝in) will form the envelope flap. 2

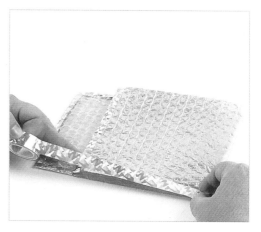

TIP

Make a bag big enough to accommodate your gift with plenty of room to spare. Fill it with more bubble wrap cut into strips, to help cushion and obscure your gift.

Seal the envelope with a piece of hologram tape, a mirrored shape, a sticker, a coin or a bow.

TIP

Pierce the outer row of bubbles to create flatter seams.

3 Bind the edges of the flap and the opposite end of the bag with the hologram adhesive tape, sticking half to the front and folding half round to the reverse. Then stick the front and back layers together down the sides to form the bag shape, this time binding both layers together. Your bubble wrap envelope is now ready to be filled.

Making a bubble wrap bag

This is better for larger presents

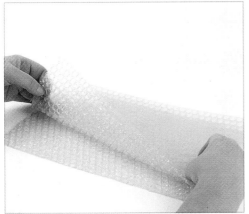

1 Cut a piece of bubble wrap. Its width should measure at least the width plus the depth of the present, while the length should be twice the height plus the depth of the present, with an additional allowance of one-third as much again so that the top can be tied. With the right side facing upward, fold the bubble wrap in half across its width.

YOU WILL NEED

bubble wrap

craft knife

cutting board

metal ruler

adhesive tape

curling ribbon

metallic pen

Don't leave the top edge of your bag unfinished. Bind it with holographic tape or stick on sequins as alternative edgings.

Bind the front and back layers together down the sides with adhesive tape. Stick half of the tape along the edge of the front then fold the other half round and press it along the edge of the back. 2

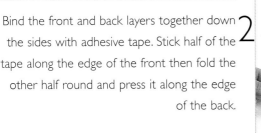

Carefully turn the bag right side out. 3

4 Finish off the top edge of your bubble wrap bag by cutting outside the line of the bubbles themselves. On the reverse side, colour in the top row of bubbles with a metallic pen. Fill the bag with packing, add your gift, then tie the top with strips of curling ribbon.

Corrugated Card

Corrugated card is a versatile and practical material that makes sturdy packaging and provides cushioning for whatever it encloses. The ridges in its construction make it strong, flexible and, at the same time, light in weight. The flute sizes vary from chunky to very fine and the different scales combine well together.

• PRINTING ON BROWN PAPER WITH CORRUGATED SHAPES CREATES NATURAL WRAPPING PAPER WITH A MODERN TWIST

• BY RUNNING IN DIFFERENT DIRECTIONS THE RIDGES OF THE CARDBOARD CREATE INTERESTING 'LOG CABIN' TEXTURES

• BUILD ON THE NATURAL TEXTURE AND COLOUR OF CORRUGATED CARD BY USING NATURAL OBJECTS, LIKE THIS FEATHER, TO CREATE ORIGINAL GIFT WRAPPING

• TOP A BOTTLE CUSHIONED IN CORRUGATED CARD WITH A NATURAL-LOOK BOW

• ROLL A MAGAZINE WITH CORRUGATED CARD AND HANDMADE PAPER TO GIVE A GIFT MAGAZINE SUBSCRIPTION MORE IMPACT

Making a pillow-shaped box
This style takes full advantage of the look that corrugated cardboard creates

YOU WILL NEED

medium weight
corrugated cardboard

scrap of chunky
corrugated cardboard

a feather

double sided adhesive
tape

craft knife

metal ruler

cutting mat

scissors

scoring tool

pencil

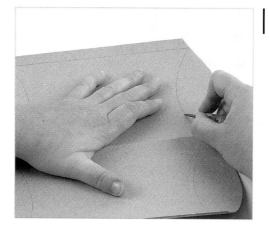

1 Copy the template on page 104, scaling it up as required. Transfer the template to the reverse of your corrugated card, taking care to position it in the correct direction in relation to the ridges. Cut it out using a craft knife and metal ruler for the straight edges and scissors for the curves. Working on the reverse of the paper, lightly score the fold lines shown on the template and create a valley fold where there is a dashed line *(see page 99).*

2 Cover the face of the side join flap with double-sided adhesive tape and press it in place under the side edge of the panel at the opposite side; be sure to align the side, top and bottom edges.

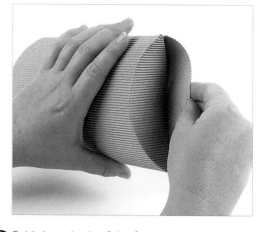

TIP

Corrugated card is only flexible across the ridges.

3 Fold down both of the flaps on one end so that they sit on top of each other and push out the sides to form a rounded shape. Decorate the front of your box, and it is ready to be filled. To close it, fold down the flaps at the other end in the same way.

Making a corrugated box

A natural packing material like feathers or raffia will suit these boxes

Measure the dimensions of the top and sides of the box lid and the parts of the box base that are visible when the lid is on. Make paper templates for each area. Position the templates on the card with the ridges running in the correct direction. To create the chequered effect on the lid, cut the template for the lid top in quarters and lay them diagonally across the ridges.

YOU WILL NEED:

a lidded box

chunky corrugated cardboard

brown paper

strong glue

craft knife

metal ruler

cutting mat

pencil

masking tape

2 Cut out all the pieces of card and stick them to the surfaces of the box with strong glue.

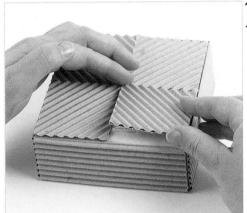

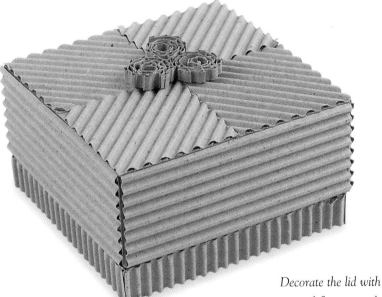

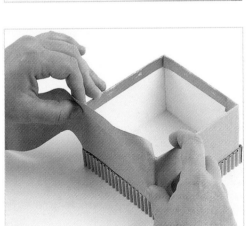

3 Cover the area where the lid overlaps the base of the box with brown paper, then decorate the lid of the box. Your box is now ready to be filled.

TIP

Mark the direction of the ridges lightly in pencil on the paper templates and on the reverse of the card to make positioning them easier.

Decorate the lid with corrugated flowers made by rolling 15cm x 7mm (6 x ½in) strips of card, into coils. Arrange them on the lid, then stick in place with strong glue.

Cardboard frames

A cardboard frame can protect and conceal the shape of a gift. Being less elaborate than a box, it is much quicker to make. You can make a plant look really stunning by presenting it in a haze of purple net, with a scalloped frame around the pot.

YOU WILL NEED

lightweight card

craft knife

metal ruler

cutting mat

scissors

double-sided adhesive
 tape

dressmaker's net

ribbon

pencil

1 Measure the overall height of the plant and pot, the circumference at the top of the plant and the circumference of the base of the pot. Make your own template the same height as the plant and half the circumference of the bottom, widening to half the circumference of the top. Curve the top edge slightly and cut scallops into it for decoration. Cut two of these shapes from the card, adding 1cm (⅜in) flaps down the sides of one piece only.

2 Apply double-sided adhesive tape to the front of the side flaps and press into place on the reverse of the side edges of the other piece, aligning the top, bottom and side edges.

TIP

To make neat scallop shapes draw round something circular, such as the top of a jam jar.

3 Put the pot into a small plastic bag (this will help to retain the moisture), then put it inside the cardboard frame. Stand the whole thing in the centre of a square of netting, bring the net up to surround the plant and tie it centrally on top with the piece of ribbon.

For something like these glasses, cut a strip of cardboard and fold it to create a triangular frame around them. Cut interlocking slits to hold the two sides together at the top.

Wrapping a round present

Circular or spherical gifts can be quite a challenge to wrap, so making a box or a bag may be the easiest solution. However, if you have some lightweight paper to hand, it is possible to wrap a circular gift neatly and attractively.

YOU WILL NEED

paper

tape measure

pair of scissors

craft knife

metal ruler

cutting mat

adhesive tape

double-sided tape

1 Measure the height and diameter of your gift. Then cut a square of paper twice the height plus twice the diameter and add 1 cm (⅜in) on each side. Cut two pieces of paper to size and use them together in a double layer.

Fold the square of paper in half and then in half again. Trim the unfolded edges into an arc so that when the paper is opened out, it is roughly circular.

2

TIP

Wrapping with layers of tissue paper in contrasting colours makes opening the gift a colourful surprise.

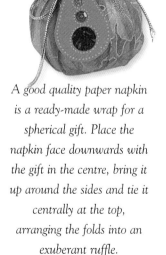

A good quality paper napkin is a ready-made wrap for a spherical gift. Place the napkin face downwards with the gift in the centre, bring it up around the sides and tie it centrally at the top, arranging the folds into an exuberant ruffle.

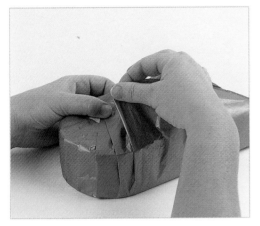

TIP

Hold the folds of paper in place temporarily with masking tape.

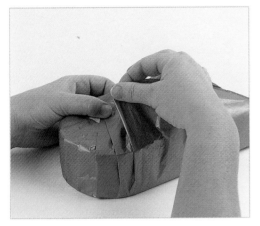

3 Place the paper face down on a flat surface and place the gift upside down in the centre. Start bringing the paper up the sides and over to the centre of the base of the gift, creating small folds to accommodate the extra paper. Work all the way round, spacing the folds as evenly as possible. Using the minimum amount of adhesive tape, stick them in place in the centre every couple of folds.

4 On the final fold turn under the end and secure it with double-sided tape (covering all the previous pieces of adhesive tape). Your parcel is now ready to be tied with ribbon. Use three separate pieces, each passed under the base of the parcel. Space them evenly around the circumference and tie them centrally on top.

A candle wrapped in tissue paper is given a magical touch with the application of glass nuggets and shimmering star trim.

Crackers

We associate crackers with the fun and laughter of celebrating Christmas and they are still a favourite Christmas tradition. However, the cracker is a very pleasing shape to use in gift wrapping at any time of the year. These crackers could contain gifts far more valuable and exciting than the usual novelty and paper hat.

CHOOSE STRONG PASTEL SHADES TO MAKE SMALL EASTER CRACKERS AND DISPLAY THEM IN ENTICING BUNDLES •

• A MODERN 3-D CHRISTMAS TREE BAND WORKS WELL IN TRADITIONAL COLOURS OF RED AND GOLD

• THIS ELEGANT CRACKER IS INSPIRED BY THE TRADITION OF DECORATING THE HOME WITH EVERGREEN FOLIAGE DURING THE FESTIVE SEASON

• THE INTERLOCKED HEART ON THIS WEDDING CRACKER CARRIES HEART-FELT WISHES FOR THE BRIDE AND GROOM

Making a wedding cracker

With their festive air, crackers are ideal for any occasion that calls for celebration

YOU WILL NEED

thin card 18 × 15cm
(7 × 5⅞in)

white giftwrap
18 × 39cm (7 × 15⅜in)

blue giftwrap
18 × 11cm (7 × 4¼in)

small pieces of white
and blue giftwrap to
make the heart

double-sided adhesive
tape

craft knife

metal ruler

cutting board

scissors

two cardboard tubes
4.5cm (1¾in) diameter
(for example, from the
centre of a kitchen roll)

two 20cm (8in) pieces
of 15mm (⅝in) ribbon

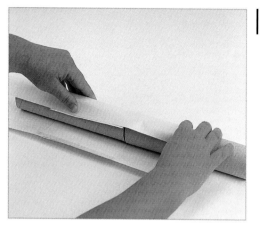

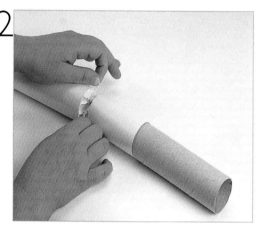

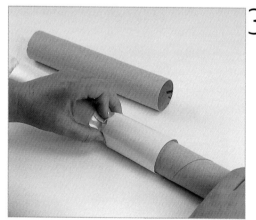

1 With the reverse side of the white giftwrap facing upwards, lay the thin card centrally on top and place the tubes across it so that their ends meet in line with the right-hand side of the piece of card. Roll the paper and card together around the tubes and secure them with double-sided adhesive tape.

2 Pull the right hand tube out slightly to create a small gap between the two tubes and tie a piece of ribbon around the 'cracker' at this point. Tie the ribbon in a double knot, gathering the paper between the two tubes. Remove the right hand cardboard tube.

3 Put your gift in from the other end, then pull the other cardboard tube out until you can feel a small gap between its inside end and the cardboard rolled up inside. Tie this end of the cracker in the gap, with the other piece of ribbon. Remove the cardboard tube. Your cracker is now ready to be decorated.

To decorate the cracker use a strip of blue giftwrap wrapped around and secured with double-sided adhesive tape and a woven paper heart.

To make the woven heart, copy the template on page 111, scaling it up as required. Transfer the template to the reverse of your two chosen papers and cut one from each with scissors. On the reverse lightly score the fold lines and create a valley fold along the dashed line *(see page 99)*.

4

The smaller crackers are made in the same way as the larger ones. The crepe paper measured 25 x 15cm (9⅞ x 5⅞in), the card 10 x 15cm (4 x 5⅞in) and a slightly narrower tube was used.

5 With the pieces folded in half, weave the strips from the two pieces through each other. Work gradually across the heart so that the strips lie alternately between and around each other.

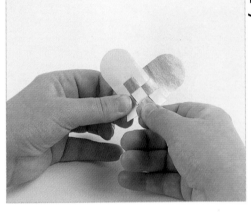

The two halves should end up at right angles to each other forming a heart-shaped envelope with two interwoven layers. Cut out a slightly smaller heart-shaped piece of paper to write your message on and put it inside.

6

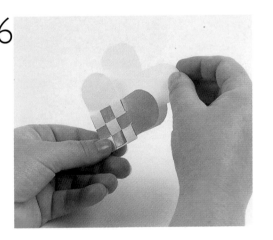

The Christmas cracker was decorated with paper ivy motifs cut from green paper using the template on page 110. Apply glue to one side. Take a 30cm(12in) length of green garden twine and lay it across the centre fold line on the leaf. Bring the two glued sides together, matching up the edges, and trapping the twine between them. Space the leaves every 4–5cm(2in) along the length of the string, then wrap it in a spiral around the cracker. Tie the ends to the string used to gather the cuffs at each end.

Woven paper baskets

Large or small, a basket is a good way to present collections of gifts. This cheering 'get well' present is easy to make and serves as a bowl while the fruit is being eaten.

YOU WILL NEED

card

tissue paper

spray adhesive

glue

craft knife

metal ruler

cutting mat

pegs

pencil

scoring tool

Create a textured effect by crumpling a piece of tissue paper and sticking it to plain card using spray adhesive *(see page 52)*. Copy the templates on page 109 scaling them up as required. Transfer them to the reverse of the card and cut them out. Lightly score all the fold lines shown and create a valley fold where there is a dashed line *(see page 99)*.

TIP

Use shredded tissue paper to present and cushion the contents.

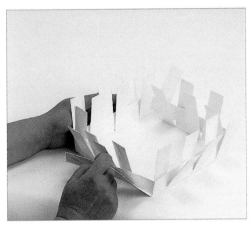

2 With the base flat on the work surface and the strips folded up to a vertical position, weave one of the loose strips (textured side out) alternately in front then behind the vertical strips. Line up the pre-folded corners with the corners of the square. Stick the beginning of the strip to the end, overlapping them to the dotted line.

Any child would love to receive this small brightly coloured basket filled with sweets. The loose strips are cut from card of a contrasting colour to create a chequered effect.

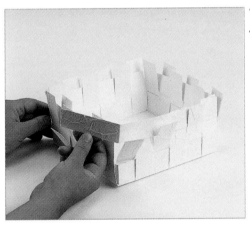

3 Weave a second strip in the same way, this time going behind the vertical strips that the previous one went in front of, and so on.

TIP

These baskets are also ideal for presenting toiletries.

Cover the reverse side of the third strip with glue and with it folded in half lengthways, press it into place, enclosing the ends of the vertical strips around the top of the basket. Again, overlap the ends to the dotted line. Use sprung clothes pegs to hold the strip in position until it is securely stuck. Your basket is now ready to be filled.

4

Tags and Embellishments

Gift tags are an integral part of decorative gift wrapping. They are also an essential means of identifying the giver, particularly at weddings, parties and Christmas. They create an opportunity to send a personal message or greeting, and if your message is very personal you can put the tag in a miniature envelope (see page 67). There is a wide range of ready-made tags available to co-ordinate with giftwraps. If you're short of time, use pre-cut blanks and decorate them with pressed flowers, decoupage or stickers for a hand-made look. (See pages 110 and 111 for templates)

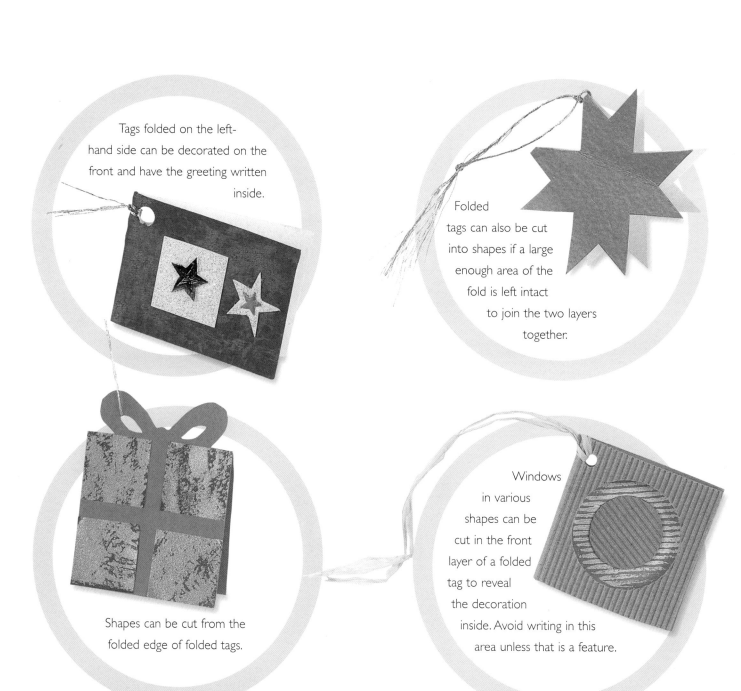

Tags folded on the left-hand side can be decorated on the front and have the greeting written inside.

Folded tags can also be cut into shapes if a large enough area of the fold is left intact to join the two layers together.

Shapes can be cut from the folded edge of folded tags.

Windows in various shapes can be cut in the front layer of a folded tag to reveal the decoration inside. Avoid writing in this area unless that is a feature.

A flat, single-layered tag like a parcel tag can be decorated on one side and have the greeting written on the reverse.

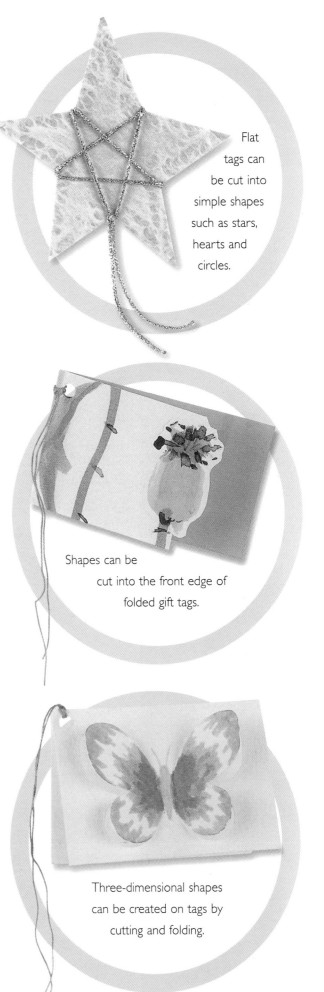

Flat tags can be cut into simple shapes such as stars, hearts and circles.

Make the fold along the top if it suits your design better.

Shapes can be cut into the front edge of folded gift tags.

Gift tags can be folded at both edges with two front flaps that meet in the middle. As with a single-fold tag, these can have shapes cut into both the edges and folds.

Three-dimensional shapes can be created on tags by cutting and folding.

Decorated tags

Here are some of the ways in which you can decorate gift tags. Keep even the smallest scraps of decorative paper, including sweet wrappers, and collect together a selection of small, lightweight objects, both natural and man-made, to use as embellishments.

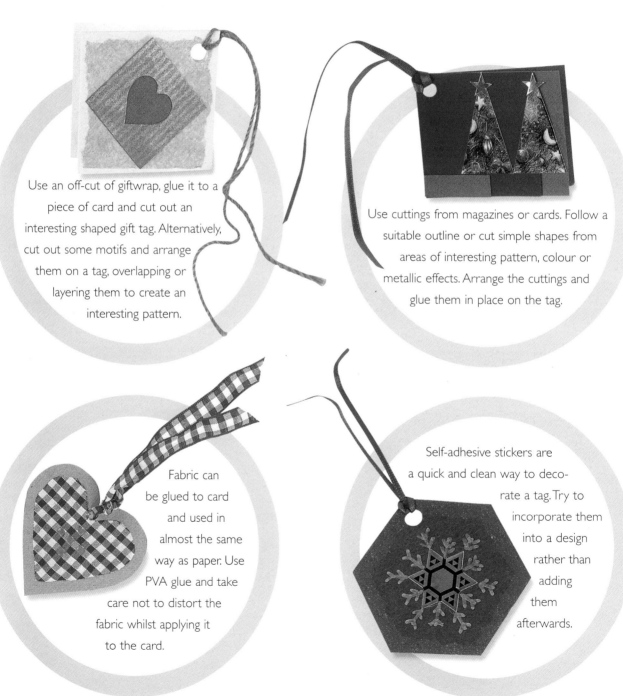

Use an off-cut of giftwrap, glue it to a piece of card and cut out an interesting shaped gift tag. Alternatively, cut out some motifs and arrange them on a tag, overlapping or layering them to create an interesting pattern.

Use cuttings from magazines or cards. Follow a suitable outline or cut simple shapes from areas of interesting pattern, colour or metallic effects. Arrange the cuttings and glue them in place on the tag.

Fabric can be glued to card and used in almost the same way as paper. Use PVA glue and take care not to distort the fabric whilst applying it to the card.

Self-adhesive stickers are a quick and clean way to decorate a tag. Try to incorporate them into a design rather than adding them afterwards.

Sequins always add a little bit of glamour. They come in a whole range of sizes and shapes such as hearts or stars, and even wordings, such as Happy Birthday.

Adhesive pads will raise an image above the surface of the tag whilst sticking it securely in place. For best results the image should be on heavy paper or light-weight card.

Pierced holes can be used to decorate gift tags *(see page 59 for instructions)*. Work directly on the tag or decorate a piece of paper separately and mount it on the tag.

Pierce or punch holes in a card shape then sew through them with string, raffia or cord to create a stitched pattern. Mount the shape on a separate piece of card to cover the reverse side of the stitching.

Pressed flowers, grasses and leaves, seed heads and feathers are beautiful natural materials to decorate tags for parcels wrapped with natural papers.

Keep a little piece of ribbon back to decorate the gift tag. Cover a tag with a strip of ribbon or decorate with shapes cut from patterned ribbon.

Paper fan bow

A quickly made fan is a smart alternative to a ribbon bow

YOU WILL NEED

19 × 24cm (7½ × 9½in) of paper

2 × 5cm (¾ × 2in) strip of paper to bind the centre

double-sided adhesive tape

pencil and ruler

scoring tool

1 Take the larger of the two pieces of paper and on the reverse side, mark lightly in pencil every 1.5cm (⅝in) along both of the longer edges. Lightly score a line between the marks, across the width of the paper.

2 Fold the paper along the scored lines concertina-style, alternately into a mountain and then a valley fold (see page 99).

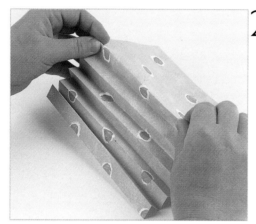

Bind the centre with the small strip of paper, overlapping its ends by about 1cm (⅜in) and secure it with a piece of double-sided tape. 3

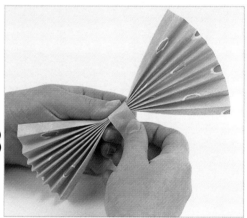

> ## TIP
>
> *Use paper in a contrasting colour to bind the centre of the bow or bind it at one end to create a larger, single fan shape.*

Decorative bundle

A pretty adornment that the recipient will want to keep

1 Cover the honesty and pine cones with a light coating of gold spray paint, following the manufacturer's directions.

YOU WILL NEED

assorted natural
   materials, such as
   honesty seedheads and
   pine cones

fine gold wire

wire cutters

gold spray paint

beads

pencil

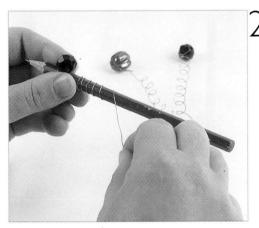

2 To make a series of beaded coils, cut some pieces of wire 30cm (12in) long. Thread a bead onto the end of each piece, twisting the wire back on itself to anchor it in place. From the bead downwards, wrap the wire around a pencil leaving 5cm (2in) straight at the other end, then slip the pencil out of the centre of the coil.

3 Arrange the honesty and the beaded coils in a fan shape and wire them together; then wire the pine cones in place at the base of the fan. Leave two 5cm (2in) ends of wire loose on the back of the arrangement to attach it to your gift.

Paper flowers

When you've perfected your technique, experiment with making lots of small flowers

YOU WILL NEED

4.5cm x 1m
   (1¾ x 39½in) strip of
   crepe paper

4.5cm x 50cm
   (1¾ x 19 ¾in) strip
   of tissue paper

scissors

adhesive stick

needle and thread

adhesive tape

1 Make the centre of the flower. Cut halfway across the width of the strip of tissue paper to create a fringe all along one of the edges. Apply adhesive to the reverse of the uncut area and roll it up all along its length.

2 Make the petals. Cut scallops along one of the edges of the crepe paper strip every 6cm (2⅜in), to within 2cm (¾in) of the opposite side. This is most easily done by folding the strip every 6cm (2⅜in) then cutting through all of the layers. Sew a line of running stitch along the base of the scallops, anchoring the thread well with a knot and adhesive tape. Gather up the strip to a length of 20cm (7⅞in) and secure the other end of the thread with a knot and adhesive tape.

3 Apply glue all along one side of the gathered edge of the crepe paper strip, then wrap it in a spiral around the base of the tissue paper roll, pressing it in place firmly.

Paper tassel

A paper tassel is an elegant finishing touch to a simple tie

1 Make a series of cuts halfway across the width of the wider paper strip, creating a fringe along one of the edges.

YOU WILL NEED

one strip of paper
6 × 12cm
(2⅜ × 4¾in)

two strips of paper
3cm × 12cm
(1⅛ × 4¾in)

piece of string

scissors

adhesive stick

Apply adhesive to one side of both the narrow strips and stick them to the reverse of the uncut area of the fringed strip, one on top of the other. 2

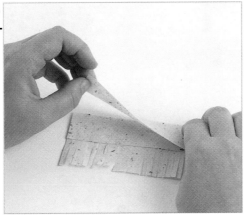

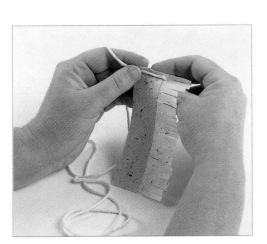

3 Apply adhesive to the reverse of the layered area then lay the piece of string across it at one end of the strip with the end of the string in line with the top of the fringed area. Roll up the strip, all along its length, trapping the string in the centre. Your tassel is now complete. Make one for each end of the string then tie it around your parcel.

Materials and Tools

In addition to the papers and cardboard, there are some tools and materials that you will need to help you achieve a professional finish to your wrapping. The first absolute necessity is a clear, flat surface to work on. It may need protecting with newspaper and it must be properly lit.

Tools

Only basic tools are needed for gift wrapping and they are very easy to use. You probably have a number of them around the house already.

CLEAR RULER is essential for accurate measurement.

TAPE MEASURE will be needed to measure around a parcel to calculate how much paper is needed to wrap it.

SHARP PENCIL will be constantly in use to mark measurements accurately, transfer templates, etc, along with a pencil sharpener and rubber.

SELECTION OF PAINTBRUSHES in different sizes are needed for applying paint or adhesive; a brush with acrylic bristles is essential for painting with bleach.

SCISSORS are indispensable for cutting around curves. A small pair is useful for intricate work and a larger pair will be needed for general use, such as cutting adhesive tape or paper. Keep a third pair exclusively for cutting ribbon as paper blunts the blades.

PINKING SCISSORS create a zigzag edge; other specialist hobby scissors create more fancy effects, for example scallop and deckle edges.

CRAFT KNIVES with retractable blades are used with a ruler to cut

straight edges from paper and card. Smaller scalpel knives are needed for intricate work such as cutting stencils. This type of knife should have a safety cap to cover the blade when not in use. Replace the blades regularly to ensure clean cuts and especially before cutting delicate papers.

CUTTING MAT of some type is essential when using a knife, to protect the work surface. A self-healing mat provides a stable base to cut on and the texture of the mat's surface prevents papers slipping and extends the life of the blade. Guide lines marked on it are very useful for cutting parallel lines and right angles.

METAL RULER is needed when cutting straight lines with a craft knife. Draw the blade along the edge of the ruler to achieve a smooth and accurate cut. A 61cm (24in) metal ruler will serve as a cutting edge and will also be useful for taking longer measurements.

HOLE PUNCH is used to make holes in tags for threading ribbon or cord, but it can also be used to create decorative holes in paper.

STAPLER is used to join multiple layers of papers together. The visible metal strips restrict its use to areas where it will not be seen or where it is used as a decorative feature.

BRADAWL is a small pointed instrument used to pierce the holes in decorative pierced designs.

SCORING TOOL is any instrument used to score along a fold line, to weaken but not break the fibres of the paper. This could be a number of things, for example a blunt tool or a knitting needle.

PAINT ROLLER is a small, rotating, foam-covered drum used to apply an even coating of paint to decorative stamps and can also be used to apply paint directly to paper.

Adhesives

Adhesives are used to stick paper and cardboard during construction and for decorative purposes. Some different glues produce a similar result so it can be a matter of personal preference which you choose. To get the best results and also for safety reasons, always follow the manufacturer's instructions for use.

STICKY TAPE is useful for permanent sticking where it will not be seen or for rough purposes such as sticking together the photocopied parts of a large template.

MASKING TAPE is used to keep papers, stencils or tracings temporarily in position. Use low tack masking tape so as not to damage the surface of delicate papers.

DOUBLE-SIDED TAPE is a strong and clean way of sticking invisibly. It has a waxed paper backing and comes on a roll so that the required length can be cut. The exposed side is applied to one layer of paper, the waxed backing peeled off, and the tape brought into contact with the second layer.

DOUBLE-SIDED FOAM ADHESIVE PADS are supplied on a sheet of waxed backing paper with another piece of waxed paper covering the other side. They can be used to create a 3D effect on gift tags as the foam raises the image away from the background.

STICK ADHESIVE is clean, safe and easy to use. It is ideal for sticking small areas of paper and card.

SPRAY ADHESIVE gives a light, even application of glue over a small or large area from an aerosol. It is ideal

for delicate papers and laminating two papers together as it does not soak or wrinkle the paper or card. Some spray adhesives allow for repositioning and a light application can be used to position stencils. Apply it in a well ventilated area and wear a mask to prevent breathing in the tiny particles of airborne adhesive.

PVA GLUE is a cheap, commonly used adhesive. It is white, but dries quite quickly to a clear, waterproof finish.

ALL-PURPOSE GLUE is a clear general adhesive used on a wide variety of materials, but not plastics. Always consult the packaging to assess suitability for the job.

SYNTHETIC SIZE is a slow-drying adhesive that goes tacky after about 15 minutes; use it to attach metal leaf.

Paints

Paints are used to decorate paper and gift tags. Even a small selection will make this a productive and enjoyable part of wrapping. For safety reasons and to achieve the best results, always follow the manufacturer's instructions.

POSTER PAINT is water based and creates a matt finish. It comes in plastic pots or bottles and has a flowing consistency. It has reasonably good covering power.

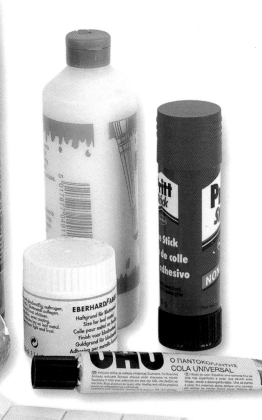

GOUACHE is a water soluble paint that is thicker than poster paint; it comes in a tube. It is more expensive but it lays down smoothly without streaking. Use it thickly for a very opaque effect or thinned with water to resemble watercolour.

SPRAY PAINT is acrylic based and dries quickly. Applied in a number of thin coats it can be used to create even colour over large areas and interesting stencil effects. Always use it outdoors or in a well-ventilated area.

PLASTIC RELIEF PAINT is used directly from the tube or bottle. You draw with it like a pen, so it is neat and clean. A wide range of colours, including metallics are available.

GLITTER GLUE is half adhesive, half 'paint'. A mix of glitter and glue is used directly from the tube or 'pen' for a real glitter effect with minimum mess.

BLEACH is used diluted one part bleach to three of water to take the colour out of tissue and crepe paper.

STENCIL AND STAMPING PAINTS are usually obtained from the same source as the stencils or stamps themselves. Ink pads are useful for small stamps, but pots of paint are required for bigger designs when the stamp is loaded with a roller.

Other materials

WAX CRAYONS can be used for rubbings and to create resist patterns on paper, as they repel water based paints.

DUTCH METAL LEAF is a cheaper version of real gold leaf. It is extraordinarily thin and quite difficult to control but it does achieve a really impressive metallic finish.

STENCIL ACETATE is a strong and durable material from which stencils are cut. Because it is transparent, positioning of motifs is made easy.

RUBBER STAMPS provide a quick and easy way of decorating with intricate designs. They are usually mounted on a wooden block with a handle to aid positioning. Some companies will do custom stamps to your own design.

FELT TIPPED PENS AND MARKERS are used to create coloured lines and the constant flow of pigment makes drawing with them fluid and clean. The width and nature of the line depends upon how fine the nib is and how it is shaped, for example conical or chisel tipped. Rubber brush tips are good for blocking in colour.

METALLIC PENS come in a variety of different nib widths and types and they are invaluable for adding fine detail or drawing small motifs in gold or silver.

Basic Techniques

measuring

Use a tape measure around three-dimensional objects and a ruler for flat measurements. Follow *either* the metric *or* imperial measurements in the projects – they are not interchangeable. Always keep a sharp point on your pencil to mark measurements with the greatest accuracy but use it lightly so that your marks can be easily erased.

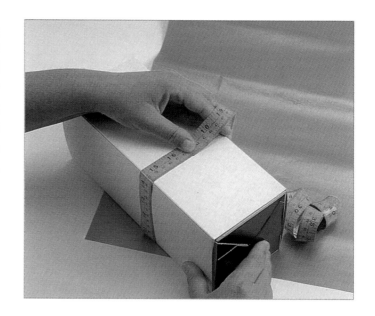

transferring a design

Take a photocopy of the relevant template from the back of the book. You can then enlarge it on a photocopier using the formula below to calculate the percentage that will increase it to the required size.

$$\frac{\text{required measurement}}{\text{actual measurement}} \times 100 = \text{percentage increase}$$

Cut out the photocopied template and using a light covering of spray adhesive or masking tape, position it on the reverse of the card or paper. Either draw round it and cut along the pencil lines, or line up the ruler with the edge of the template and cut around it. Score lines can be marked through at either end with a small indentation made with a pencil dot. If you plan to make a number of items from the same template, stick the enlarged, photocopied template to a piece of lightweight card before cutting out the shape.

Some of the motifs given at the back of the book can be used actual size to create decorative details and these can be traced. Draw the outline which you will see clearly through the tracing paper, with a pencil. To transfer a pencil line the correct way round, turn over the tracing paper and scribble on the reverse of the lines. Turn it over again, lay it on the chosen paper or card and go over the outline to transfer the image.

scoring

Use a knitting needle, the back of a blade or a bone folder, any tool that will make a groove in the paper but not pierce it. Draw it across the paper leaving an indentation. This weakens the fibres, making it easier to fold at that point. However, take care not to press too hard when scoring to avoid breaking the fibres of the paper.

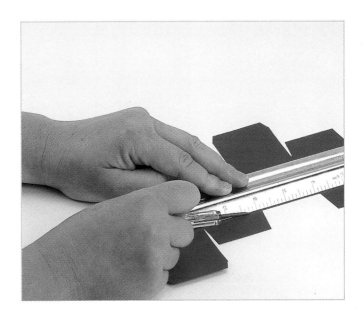

folding

Paper retains creases well and is also flexible, allowing a fold to act as a hinge that can be opened and closed. You can use a bone folder to smooth the paper, but if you keep your hands very clean, you can use just your fingers. If the paper is very fragile, put a piece of clean paper between it and your finger. On the templates, a mountain fold (which is raised) is indicated by a dotted line and a valley fold (which is indented) is indicated by a dashed line.

cutting

A cut edge is indicated by a solid line on the templates. Use a sharp blade to get a nice clean cut, but always be safe, so keep your fingers well back from the edge of the metal ruler. Keep the blade angled downwards so that you use a reasonable area of it to cut with, not just the tip. Press down firmly on the metal ruler so that it and the paper do not move. Keep the ruler in place until you have checked that the cut is clean and doesn't need a second stroke. When cutting card, two or three even strokes with uniform pressure are better than one stroke pressing very hard, possibly resulting in a faltering cut that is likely to move the metal ruler.

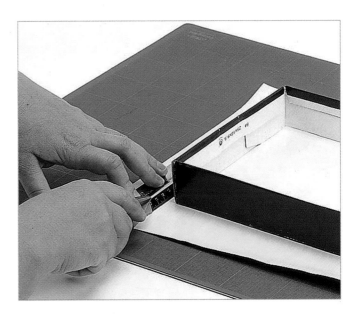

Lidded box

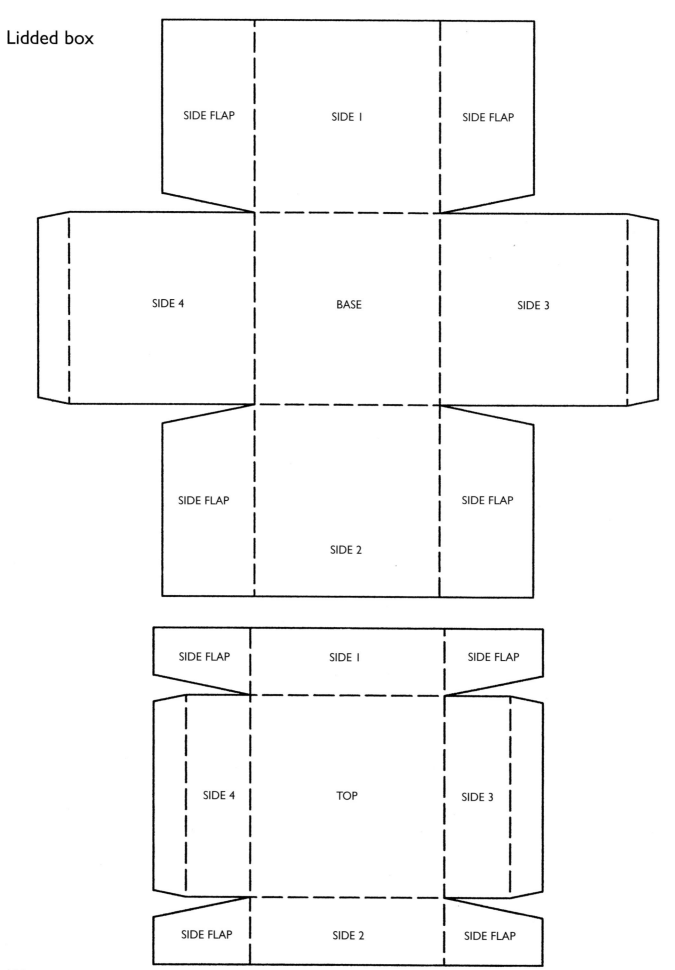

SIDE FLAP

SIDE 1

SIDE FLAP

SIDE 4

BASE

SIDE 3

SIDE FLAP

SIDE FLAP

SIDE 2

SIDE FLAP

SIDE 1

SIDE FLAP

SIDE 4

TOP

SIDE 3

SIDE FLAP

SIDE 2

SIDE FLAP

Hinged box

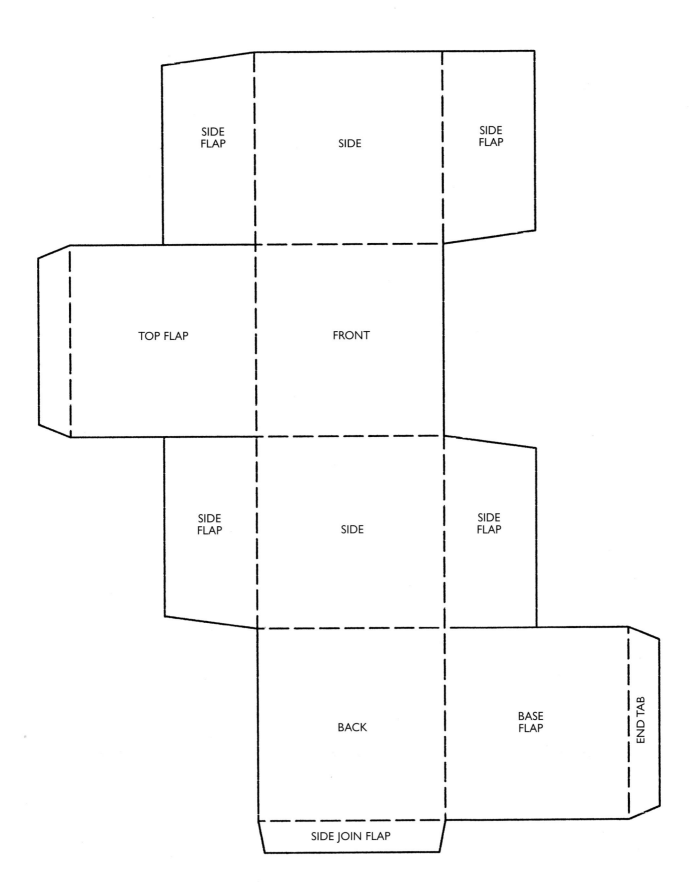

SIDE FLAP

SIDE

SIDE FLAP

TOP FLAP

FRONT

SIDE FLAP

SIDE

SIDE FLAP

BACK

BASE FLAP

END TAB

SIDE JOIN FLAP

Self closing box

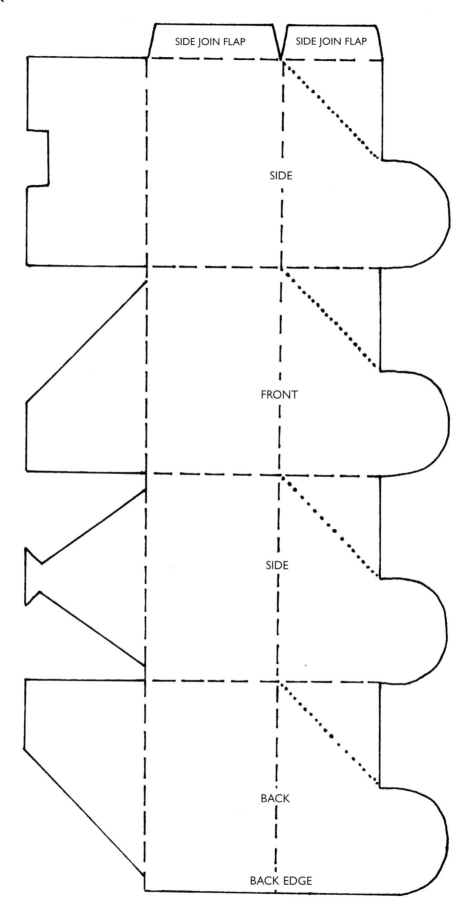

SIDE JOIN FLAP SIDE JOIN FLAP

SIDE

FRONT

SIDE

BACK

BACK EDGE

Paper bag

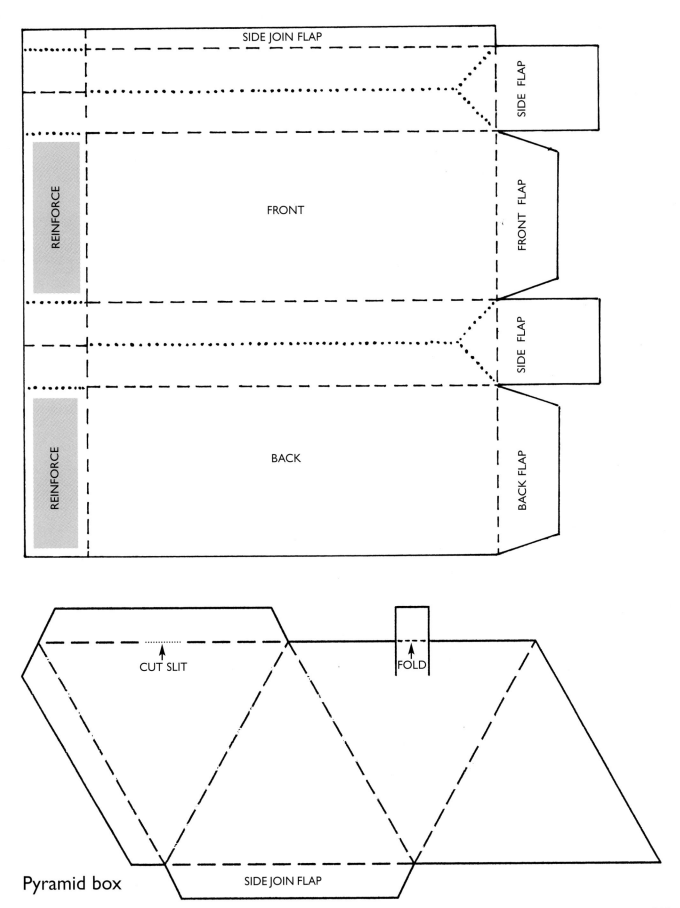

SIDE JOIN FLAP

SIDE FLAP

REINFORCE

FRONT

FRONT FLAP

SIDE FLAP

REINFORCE

BACK

BACK FLAP

CUT SLIT

FOLD

Pyramid box

SIDE JOIN FLAP

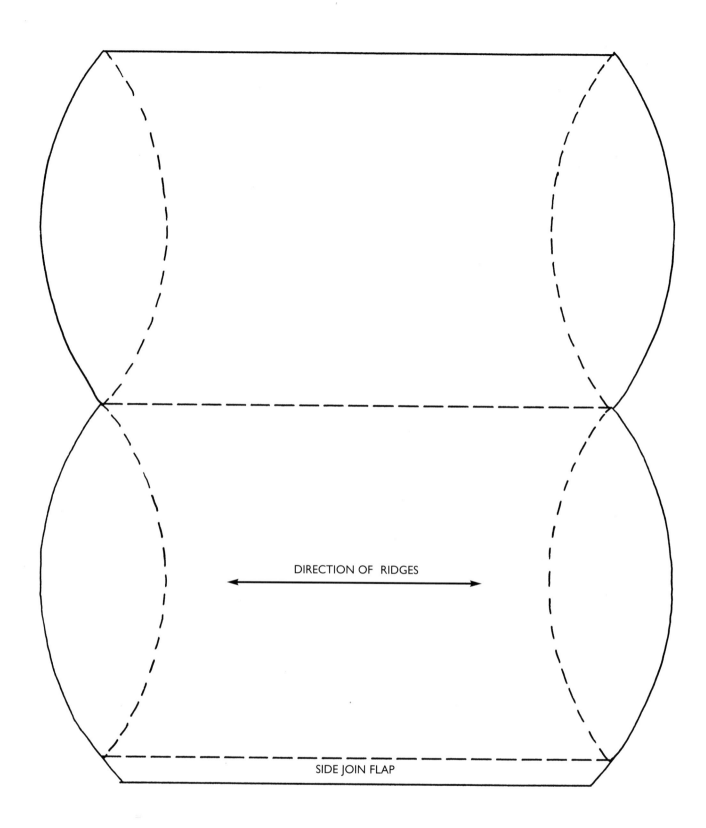

DIRECTION OF RIDGES

SIDE JOIN FLAP

Pillow box

Hexagonal box

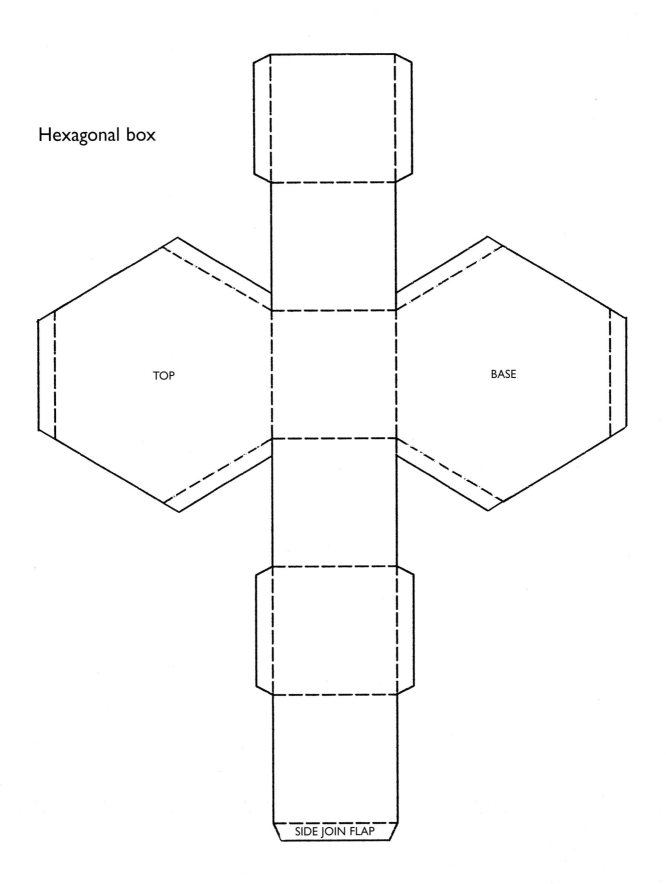

TOP

BASE

SIDE JOIN FLAP

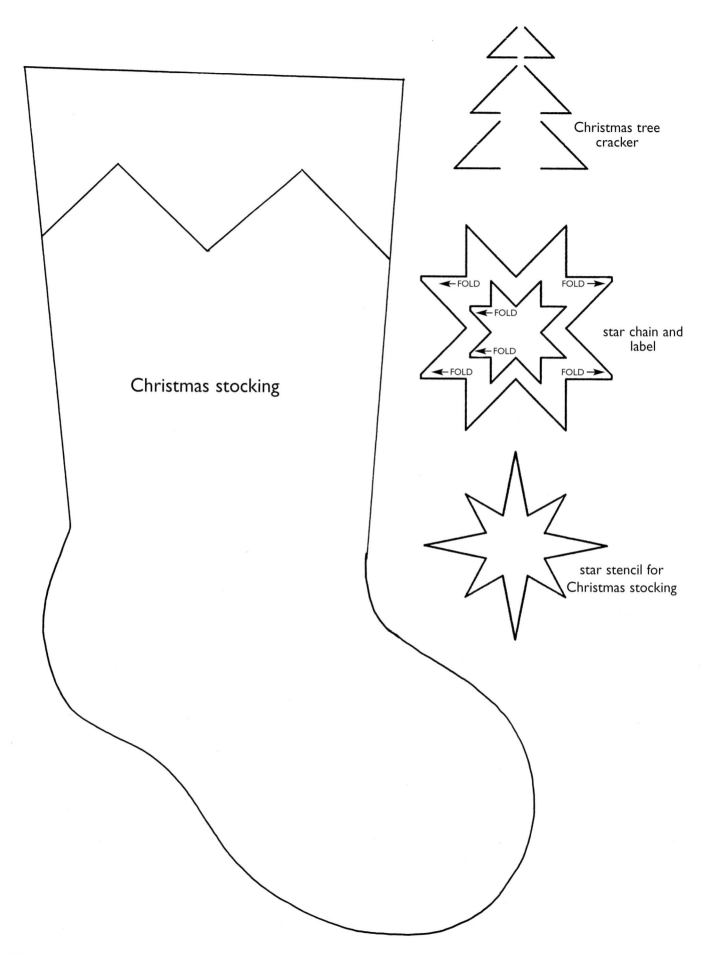

Christmas tree
cracker

Christmas stocking

FOLD   FOLD
FOLD
star chain and
label
FOLD
FOLD   FOLD

star stencil for
Christmas stocking

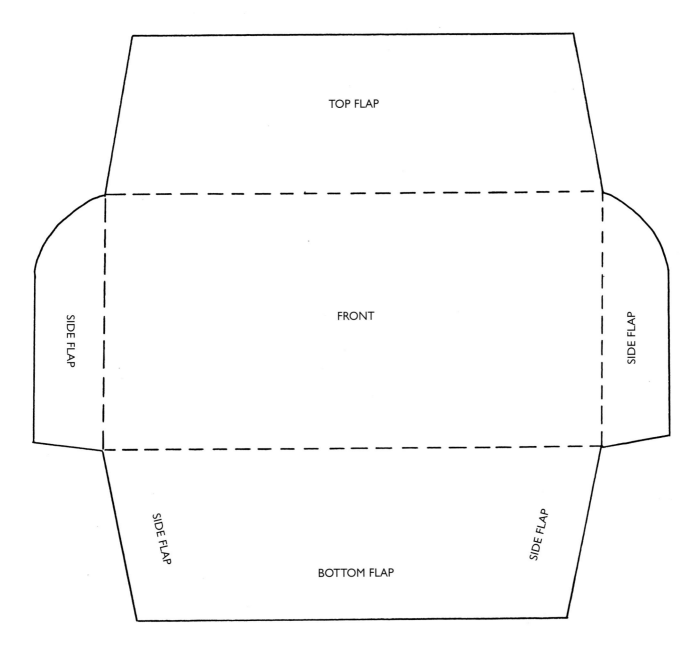

TOP FLAP

SIDE FLAP

FRONT

SIDE FLAP

SIDE FLAP

BOTTOM FLAP

SIDE FLAP

Envelope

Heart sachet

Filigree design

Pierced paisley

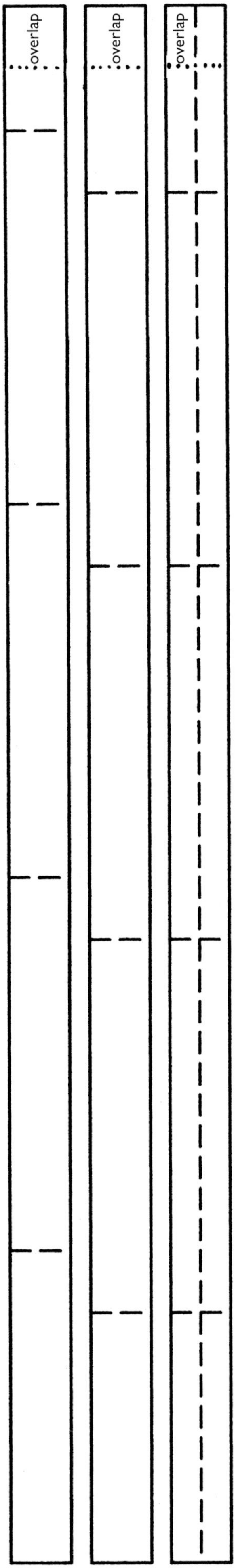

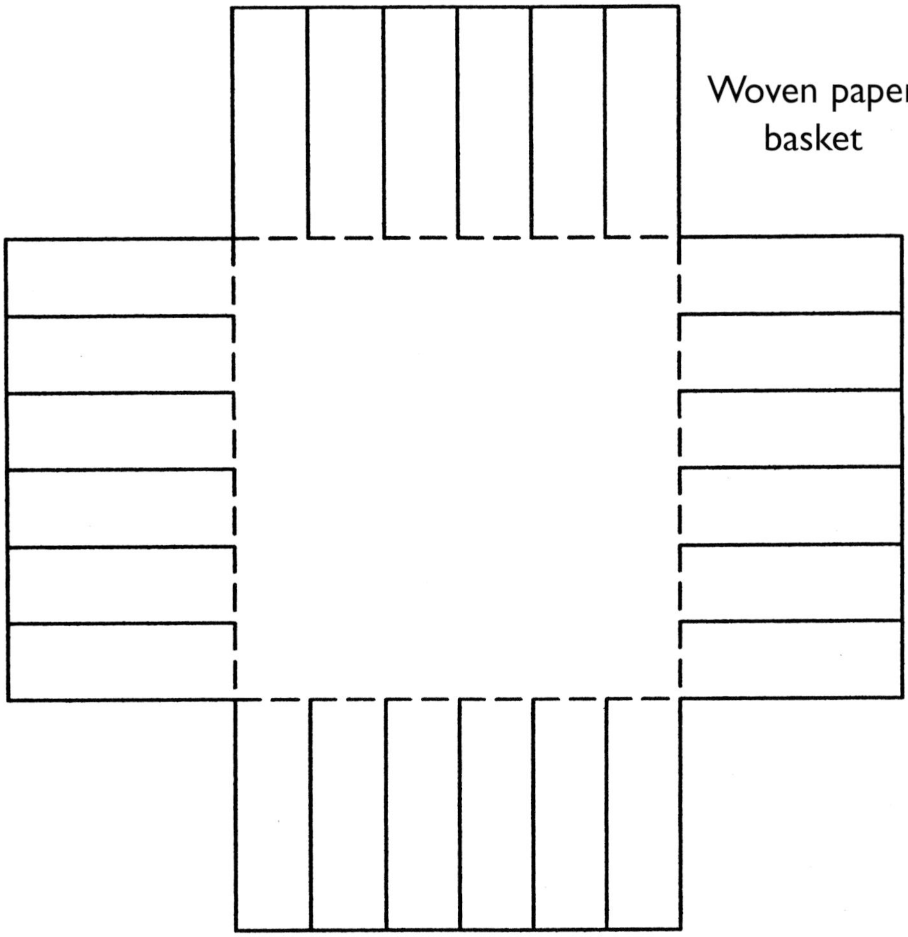

Woven paper basket

Fabric bag flower patch

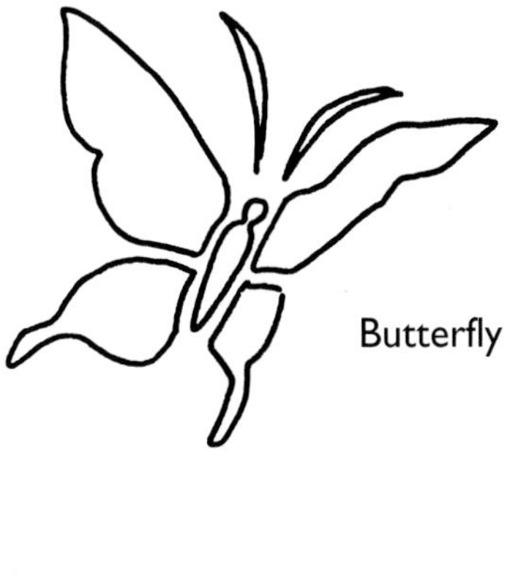

Butterfly stencil

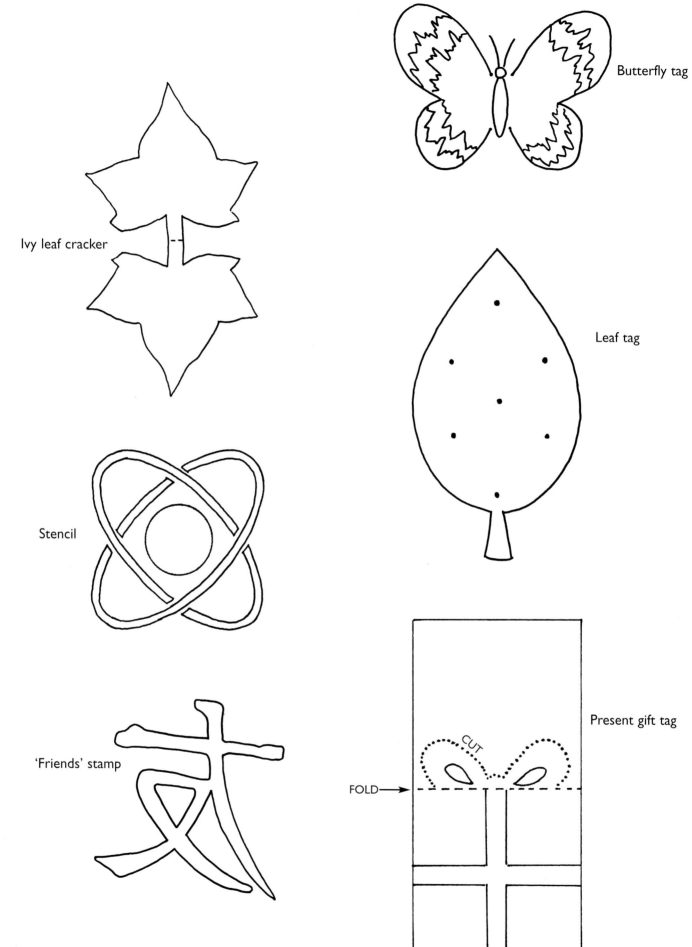

Butterfly tag

Ivy leaf cracker

Leaf tag

Stencil

'Friends' stamp

Present gift tag

CUT

FOLD→

Paper bag cut out handle

FOLD →

Woven heart

Tag shapes

Index